C

Andrew and Janet Goodwyn

Oxford University Press

Oxford University Press, Walton Street, Oxford OX2 6DP

Oxford New York
Athens Auckland Bangkok Bombay
Calcutta Cape Town Dar es Salaam Delhi
Florence Hong Kong Istanbul Karachi
Kuala Lumpur Madras Madrid Melbourne
Mexico City Nairobi Paris Singapore
Taipei Tokyo Toronto

and associated companies in
Berlin Ibadan

Oxford is a trade mark of Oxford University Press

© Selection and activities: Andrew and Janet Goodwyn 1992
Reprinted 1994

ISBN 0 19 831280 6

Typeset by Pentacor PLC, High Wycombe, Bucks
Printed and bound in Great Britain by
Butler & Tanner Ltd, Frome and London

Cover illustration by Nicky Marsh

Also available in the *Oxford Literature Resources* series:

Contemporary Stories 1	0 19 831251 2
Contemporary Stories 2	0 19 831254 7
Stories from South Asia	0 19 831255 5
Science Fiction Stories	0 19 831261 X
Fantasy Stories	0 19 831262 8
Sport	0 19 831264 4
Autobiography	0 19 831265 2
Love	0 19 831279 2
Scottish Short Stories	0 19 831281 4
American Short Stories	0 19 831282 2
Travel Writing	0 19 831283 0
Reportage	0 19 831284 9

Contents

Acknowledgements iv

Preface v

The Reluctant Detective   *Michael Z. Lewin*   1
Something the Cat Dragged In   *Patricia Highsmith*   16
Superfluous Murder   *Milward Kennedy*   37
The Man with the Twisted Lip   *Sir Arthur Conan Doyle*   52
The Case for the Defence   *Graham Greene*   77
Philomel Cottage   *Agatha Christie*   81
A Pair of Yellow Lilies   *Ruth Rendell*   104
A Wife in a Million   *Val McDermid*   116
The Necklace of Pearls   *Dorothy L. Sayers*   126
Activities   137
Extended Activities   153
Wider Reading   154

Acknowledgements

The editors and publishers are grateful for permission to include the following copyright stories in this collection.

Agatha Christie, 'Philomel Cottage' from *The Listerdale Mystery*. Copyright © 1934 Agatha Christie Mallowan. Reprinted by permission of Aitken & Stone Ltd. **Graham Greene**, 'The Case for the Defence' from *Collected Stories* (Wm Heinemann Ltd. & The Bodley Head Ltd.). Reprinted by permission of Laurence Pollinger Ltd. on behalf of the Estate of Graham Greene. **Patricia Highsmith**, 'Something the Cat Dragged In' from *Black House*. Reprinted by permission of William Heinemann Limited, first published in *Verdict of Thirteen*, A Detection Club Anthology, (Faber, 1979). Copyright © 1979 by Patricia Highsmith. All rights reserved. **Milward Kennedy**, 'Superfluous Murder' from *Great Tales of Detection*, ed. Dorothy L. Sayers. Reprinted by permission of J. M. Dent & Sons Ltd. Publishers. **Michael Z. Lewin**, 'The Reluctant Detective', reprinted in *The Mammoth Book of Modern Crime Stories*, ed. George Hardinge (Robinson Publishing, 1987). © Macmillan, London 1986. **Val McDermid**, 'A Wife in a Million' from **Reader, I Murdered Him**, ed. Jen Green (The Women's Press Ltd.). Copyright Val McDermid. Reprinted by permission of Gregory & Radice, Authors' Agents. **Ruth Rendell**, 'A Pair of Yellow Lilies' from Ellery Queen's Mystery Magazine, April 1989. Reprinted by permission of Peters Fraser & Dunlop Ltd. **Dorothy L. Sayers**, 'A Necklace of Pearls' from *Hangman's Holiday* (NEL, 1974). Reprinted by permission of David Higham Associates.

Every effort has been made to secure all permissions prior to publication. However in one instance this has not proved possible. If contacted the publisher will be pleased to rectify any errors or omissions at the earliest opportunity.

Preface

You might think that most people have criminal tendencies because crime is so popular, or rather fictional crime is so popular. Is there anyone who does not have some idea, however vague, of who Sherlock Holmes is? At the moment you read this, there will be half a dozen detective series running on television in one week.

This fascination seems to be partly attributable to our human interest in motives. What makes someone actually take the terrible decision to murder another human being? Or, on a more ordinary level, why would an old-age pensioner take a tin of beans from the supermarket? The criminal impulse seems to concern everyone.

There is also the simple but vital point that we become the detective as we read these stories. We, as readers, can solve the crime. We know that the author has supplied us with all the clues, has perhaps set up some misleading evidence, and has given us a number of suspects. We ask and answer the old question, 'Who done it?' and usually we are left admiring the incredible deductive skill of the fictional detective and the amazing ingenuity of the writer. In solving the crime, however it is done, our sense of justice is usually awakened; we are satisfied with having solved the puzzle of the crime and also because justice is done.

In spite of our concern with justice, however, we are also liberated by the detective story because it gives us the chance to be both detective and criminal. The question we ask is therefore not 'Who done it?', but 'Will they get away with it?'. Crime stories then are not just about robberies and murders: they reveal the difficulties we all have in telling the good guys from the bad guys. They concern the fact that we are all a bit of both.

Crime, of course, is as old as the human race and stories about it have a long history. You can find plenty of examples in old legends of highwaymen and ghosts of murdered souls. In Victorian times as the police became a national force, prisons as we know them were introduced, so crime became an everyday matter, reported in all the papers, and occupying an increasingly large space on the fiction shelf of every library. With the appearance of Conan Doyle's Sherlock Holmes came the type of stories that we now call detective fiction.

This collection aims to bring you an interesting mixture of some of the best examples of the genre. We have included perhaps the two most famous writers, Conan Doyle and Agatha Christie, but also a range of other writers. The crimes vary from murder to theft and poisoning and the detectives range from the brilliant to the reluctant.

The follow on activities provide an extensive range of work both spoken and written. Anyone working through the collection would cover many of the requirements of GCSE and of Key Stage Four.

Finally we hope that the collection will inspire readers by presenting them with material that they really want to read but that is also thought-provoking and challenging.

The Reluctant Detective

Michael Z. Lewin

It started as a tax fiddle. Well, paint on a little semantic gloss: call it a tax avoidance structurization. Uncle Edward would have preferred that, I think.

It was Uncle Edward who was responsible for my coming to England in the first place. I am American by birth and by upbringing. So was he, but some time in his relative youth he moved over here – I don't know what brought him – and he stayed. That was a long time ago, his moving. Before I was born. I'm twenty-six now. And I never actually met him, though I wrote to him often. Not letters exactly, because what we did was play postal chess. We did that over a period of more than ten years, so while I didn't know him at all, I felt I knew him fairly well. You get a sense of people by their chess games. Look at Anatoly Karpov's style on the board and you'll see a map of his face. No expression in either.

But that's by the by, I was Uncle Edward's only child-age relative – he never had kids of his own – and from the time I was born he kept in contact. He was quite close to his sister – my mother – and I always got a present on my birthday and at Christmas. It added a certain cosmopolitan touch to these occasions. And then he wrote direct to me when he heard from Mom that I had begun to play with the chess set he sent. We took it from there, playing by post till he died. Even during my years in college we kept it up. And afterwards too, when I was realizing I didn't want to be a lawyer, no matter what Dad said about it being useful to fall back on even if I didn't know what I *really* wanted to do.

When Uncle Edward died I was sad. He was one of my few fixed points, a focus for a little contemplative time no matter where I was or what a shambles I was making of the rest of my life.

1

When I learned that Uncle Edward had provided for me in his will, I was astonished.

What I inherited was a house over here. Also a small income to be sent to me every month from the States. Just about enough to live on.

At first I didn't know what to do. Sell the house, or what. But when I thought about it, it occurred to me that if I thought I could tell about Uncle Edward from our chess games, maybe he could tell about me. Perhaps he was suggesting that it would be good for me to live in England for a while. I'm sure he knew from Mom that I was kind of at loose ends anyway because they wrote to each other. Actual letters, I mean. She only ever quoted to me from one once. When I asked her why Uncle Edward lived in England. She said he had written, *Britain is the closest thing there is left to a civilized English-speaking country.* 'He was never very good at languages,' she said after. The more I thought about it the better an idea it seemed. So I decided to give it a try, and over I came.

The tax fidd . . . tax avoidance structurization didn't come up till I had been here a year or so. In fact, it was Dawn's idea, so in a way everything that's happened is down to to her.

Dawn is the lady friend I've made. She is very civilized and if she is what Uncle Edward meant, I understand better why he spent his life here. It could happen to me, though that's not something I think about a lot.

Dawn agreed to move in after I'd been here about six months. We live in my house, and on my income. It gives us a lot of time to enjoy life. And think about things. We're not quite what they call drop-outs back home, because we intend to get into careers when we're sure what we want to do. But if we have no need to rush a decision . . . well, we didn't make the rules.

I see I'm already talking as if I am staying forever. Well, there are worse fates.

And, it turns out, we've already done something along a career line, even if it was strictly by accident. That's what this story is about.

OK, get the picture. I come over here to my house and an income. After six months Dawn and I are friends enough to live together. After six months we realize that comfortable as my income is, maybe there are things it would be nice to do if there was a little more money around.

Get a car for one. Nothing flash, but some wheels to see some of the rest of the country with.

Have I told you where I am? It's a little town in Somerset called Frome. (They pronounce it to rhyme with broom, by the way.) And it is pretty enough and in a lovely part of the country. But there are other places to see. Yes, it was considering getting a car that set us thinking in the first place.

Or set Dawn thinking, actually. She is the one who cooked it all up.

The idea was this. If I set up in business, as a self-employed person I could save money in taxes by deducting a lot of what we spent as necessary commercial expenses. Part of the house as an office; proportion of rates and heat and repairs and insurance; even a salary to Dawn as my secretary. And all the costs of my business vehicle.

Dawn worked it all out, and there was no question, it would pay for the car. And maybe a little bit more as we went along.

Then the question was what kind of business to supposedly set up in. That was Dawn's idea too. Well, not all ideas are necessarily bright.

I set up as a private detective. See, in Britain you don't need a licence of any kind. And, I have to admit, we yielded to a certain pleasant absurdity attached to the notion. I mean, a private detective, in Frome!

As well, the chances of anybody coming to us for business were, of course, nil.

Which was the idea. We didn't want the business to succeed, or, indeed, for there to be any work at all. What we wanted were the deductions. It was a tax fiddle. As I've mentioned.

So, I bought a notebook and pen, and a small sign to put on the front of the house. It gave my name and under it *Private*

Inquiry Agent which is what they call private detectives here.
And that was it.

No advertisements, no listing in the Yellow Pages.

And no business.

We bought a little yellow Mini. Life as planned. It worked like a charm.

For a while.

It was a Tuesday, I remember, because I was reading the basketball column in *The Guardian* – I try to keep up with some of my old interests from the USA – when the doorbell rang. It was about ten o'clock. I thought it might be the gas man. Dawn was out visiting her mother – she's got as many relatives here as I have none, so to speak. A lot is what I am saying.

At the door was a sallow-faced little man – well, I suppose he was about average height, but I am awkwardly tall, about 6′ 5″, so I have a distorted perspective on people. He had a jacket and tie on and he looked unhappy.

I thought, not the gas man but maybe a local government official.

'Are you Mr Herring?' he asked.

'Yes.'

'May I talk to you?'

'What about?' I asked.

He looked momentarily at the sign on the house by the door. It's so small you can hardly see it even if you know it's there. 'Are you the Mr Herring who is a private inquiry agent?'

And I suddenly realized he had come on business. I was stunned. I began to shake, though I don't know if he noticed.

'Yes, yes, of course,' I said. 'Frederick Herring. Do come in.'

I led him to the living-room. It wasn't much to look at. Not for a detective's office. It was just a living-room, and lived in at that.

I sat him down. I didn't know what to say. But he made the running.

'My name is Goodrich,' he said.

'Hi.'

4

'I don't know whether I should even be here.'

'It's not a step to take lightly,' I said.

'I'm not,' he said. 'I'm not.'

'Oh.'

'I am a solicitor with Malley, Holmes and Asquith, but I need someone to make some inquiries for me on a private matter.'

'I see.'

'Well, you do that kind of thing, don't you?'

He looked at me. There was something devious in his eyes. And I had a sudden shock of suspicion.

You see, Dawn and I had talked about what to do if someone did actually come to us for work. We would just say that we were too busy to take the case on. But there was something about this man. The same thing that made me think he might be a council official. I got this idea that he was from one of the tax offices and that he was checking up on us.

It's just that on all these tax forms we'd been sending in we always had expenses listed, but never any income. It looked funny, of course. But economic times are hard and we assumed our amounts were so small, relatively, that nobody would notice.

But when you think you are being checked on, you suddenly feel the cold draught of accusation, prosecution.

'Of course,' I said.

Dawn was not pleased when she returned to the house and found that I had taken a case. But I explained my worries and she accepted the situation as a fact.

'It's about his brother-in-law, a guy named Chipperworth, who is a crook,' I said.

'Chipperworth . . . ' Dawn said. She was thinking. She's lived in Frome all her life and knows a lot of people.

'He has a company that manufactures beds, up on the trading estate. The brand name is Rest Easy.'

'Ah.'

'You know it?'

'Rest Easy, yes.'

'And this man Goodrich says that Chipperworth set fire to a warehouse next to his factory up there and collected the insurance for it.'

'I read about the fire,' Dawn said. 'But not that it was on purpose. How does Goodrich know?'

'He says Chipperworth was bragging yesterday that he had just collected a cheque for over three hundred thousand pounds and it was for beds he wasn't going to be able to sell.'

'Good heavens,' Dawn said. 'But why doesn't Goodrich go to the police?'

'Because that's not what he's trying to sort out.'

'Oh.'

'What he's worried about is his sister. That Chipperworth is a crook, and he's dangerous. He wants his sister to divorce him.'

Dawn cocked her head.

'But his sister doesn't believe the stuff about the insurance fraud.'

'What are *me* supposed to do about that?'

'Goodrich wants us to prove Chipperworth has a woman on the side. If we can do that then the sister will divorce him and will be safe. Goodrich is sure that his sister will get a divorce in the end anyway, but if he precipitates it at least she'll be well off financially. If he waits till Chipperworth's activities catch up with him then it might ruin the sister too.'

'Oh,' Dawn said.

'I agreed to try.'

She nodded. Then she looked at me.

And I looked at her.

We were thinking the same thing.

I said, 'What the hell do we do now?'

Well, we had to go through the motions. The first motion was to find Chipperworth and identify him.

That wasn't hard. Mr Goodrich had given me a photograph and we decided to wait outside Rest Easy Beds toward the end of the work day. Rest Easy was not a big company. We counted about twenty people coming out after five-thirty. Chipperworth was the last and got into a new Sierra.

'OK,' Dawn said. 'There he is. What do we do now?'

'Drive along after him, I guess,' I said.

So we did. He went straight to a house on the Prowtings Estate. He pulled the car into the driveway. Got out. Went to the front door. Was met by a woman at 5.48 p.m. Then Chipperworth went into the house and closed the door.

That would have wrapped the case up if the woman hadn't been his wife.

Dawn and I sat.

'At least we know the registration number of his car now,' I said after ten minutes.

But we were both sinking fast.

After half an hour Dawn said, 'This is no good. What are we going to do, sit out here all night without any food or anything?'

And after some consideration of the situation, we decided to get fish and chips from Pangs. Even detectives have to eat.

When we got back, Chipperworth's car was gone.

Solicitor Goodrich rang up at nine the next morning. He seemed annoyed that I didn't have anything to report.

I explained that progress is not always rapid, that we'd had less than a day on the job.

But Goodrich knew that Chipperworth had been out the previous night. He'd called his sister and she told him.

'If you want to do the surveillance yourself,' I said, 'please say so. Otherwise leave it to us.'

He took a breath, then apologized – rather unconvincingly I thought – and we hung up.

I told Dawn about the call.

'If we don't sort this out quickly,' she said, 'it's going to mess up our lives for weeks.'

'I know.'

'I'm going to see a couple of my cousins.'

I looked puzzled.

'Nigel is a telephone engineer,' she said. 'He's a nut case and would probably be willing to work out a way to tap the

Chipperworths' telephone. And Paul works in the photographic section at Valets.' Valets was one of the local printing firms. 'He's a camera buff. He'll lend us a camera with a telephoto lens.'

'Right,' I said.

'We may have to borrow another car too, so we can cover Chipperworth the whole day. If it goes on for long we'll have to do shifts. I ought to be able to use Adele's Reliant. You remember Adele?'

'No.'

'She's the small one with the big—'

'I remember now,' I said.

Biggest feet I'd ever seen on a woman.

'I just wish I knew someone who could lend us a two-way radio.'

'There's your Uncle Mike,' I said.

'So there is,' she said. Then made a face. 'But he pinches and pokes whenever I get close enough and what he'd want for doing me a favour . . .'

'We'll get along without,' I said firmly.

In the end it only took a day.

It was the afternoon of my first shift. I was rigged up with a thermos, sandwiches and a radio. Even a specimen jar – from Dawn's friend Elaine, the nurse – in case time was short and need was great.

When Dawn and I get down to it, we're impressive.

I took the afternoon shift because Dawn had to see her Auntie Wendy who was having troubles with a neighbour's boy picking on her son Edgar.

The camera was one of those instant print jobs. We'd talked it over with Paul and he figured that would be best. No time waiting for the film to come back from the developers. 'And,' he said, 'considering what kind of pictures you may get, a commercial firm might not print them.' Does a great leer, does Paul.

He also gave us a foot-long lens for the thing. 'It'll put you in their pockets,' he said. 'If they're wearing pockets.'

Cousin Nigel jumped at the chance to plant a tape recorder up a telephone pole to tap the Chipperworths' home phone. He volunteered to do the company phone too. Well, you don't turn down offers like that.

It's always struck me that all of Dawn's family are just that little bit shady. I offer it as an observation, not a complaint.

Anyway, after an hour's lunch at home, Chipperworth didn't go back to his office. He drove instead to Marston Road and pulled into the driveway of a detached brick house just beyond the end of speed restrictions. I drove past but parked immediately. I left the car and got the camera aimed and focused just in time to see Chipperworth open the door to the house with a key.

The picture came out a treat.

I stood there in the road looking at it. And wondering what to do next.

But Dawn and I had talked it through. First I made a note of the time, date and location on the back of the photograph. Then I set about trying to find out who lived in the house.

I went next door and rang the bell and had a little luck.

A tiny old woman with big brown eyes answered it. I said, 'Excuse me, I have a registered letter for the people next door but nobody answers when I ring.'

'That's because Mrs Elmitt has her fancy man in,' the old woman said. 'And she wouldn't want to be disturbed now, would she? Some of the things I've seen! And they don't even bother to draw the curtains.'

Old women can do pretty good leers too, when they try.

Dawn was pleased as punch with me. I was pretty pleased myself. It meant that the wretched case would soon be over and we could get back to life as usual. I resolved to try to arrange for my income to arrive from America as some kind of retainer so that it looked like proceeds of the business. Then we wouldn't have to worry about being inspected by the tax people. Worry is a terrible thing.

But just about the time that we were getting ready to be

pleased with each other, Cousin Nigel showed up at the front door.

He punched me on the shoulder as he came in, and gave Dawn a big kiss. A hearty type, Nigel.

'I've got your first tape,' he said jovially. 'Went up to see if it needed changing and blow me if there hadn't been a lot of calls. Thought you would want to hear them sooner rather than later, so I put another cassette in the machine and brought this one right over. Got any beer while we listen to it?' He dropped into our most comfortable chair. 'Hey Dawnie, how about something to eat? Egg and chips? Hungry work, bugging telephones.'

The tape was a revelation.

Right off, the very first phone call had things like the man saying, 'Darling, I can't wait until I see you again.'

And the woman: 'I don't know whether I'll be able to bear not being with you all the time for very much longer.'

'It will be soon. We'll be together, forever. Somewhere nice. Away from your wretched husband.'

'I don't know what will become of me if our plan doesn't work.'

'It will work. We'll make it work.'

'Oh darling, I hope so.'

And on and on, that kind of mushy stuff. There was a lot of slobbering sounds too. I would have been embarrassed if I hadn't been so upset.

'Wow!' Nigel said. 'All that kissy-kissy, and before lunch. They must have it bad.'

Dawn said, 'Isn't that great! We've got all we need now, Freddie, don't you think?'

But I was not happy, not even close.

Because, unlike my two colleagues, I had recognized one of the voices. The man's. The conversation was not between Mr Chipperworth and Mrs Elmitt. The man on the telephone was our client, Mr Goodrich, and the object of his affection was, presumably, Mrs Chipperworth, his 'sister'.

We got rid of Nigel before we talked it out.

'I guess this means that our client was not being completely open and frank with us,' Dawn said.

There was no law that a client had to tell us the truth. But neither of us liked it.

'But what do we do?'

We had a long chat about it.

What we did was go the next morning to see Dawn's Uncle Steve, who is a police sergeant. We asked him about the fire in the Rest Easy Beds warehouse.

'Always knew it was arson,' Uncle Steve said. 'But we couldn't prove who did it. The owner was the only possible beneficiary, but he had an airtight alibi. Not quite as good as being out to dinner with the Chief Superintendent, but he was at a function with the Mayor and he was at a table, in full sight, the whole evening.'

'I see,' Dawn said.

'I interviewed Chipperworth myself,' Uncle Steve said, 'and he was quite open about being delighted about the fire. Business wasn't very good and he was having trouble moving the stock that was destroyed. Personally, I don't think he *did* have anything to do with it. I've been at this job long enough to get a good sense of people and that's the way he came across.'

'I see,' Dawn said.

'But we never got so much as a whiff of any other suspect. Checked through all current and past employees for someone with a grievance. Sounded out all our informants in town for a word about anybody who might have been hired to do the deed or who heard anything about it. But we didn't get so much as a whisper. It's very unusual for us not to get some kind of lead if something's bent and we try that hard. In the end, it was written off to kids. There are so many around with nothing to do these days that we're getting all sorts of vandalism.'

'Thanks, Uncle Steve,' Dawn said.

'Help you, does that?' he asked.

'I think so.'

'If you know anything about the case, you must tell us. You know that, don't you?'

'Yes, Uncle Steve.'

He looked at her and shook his head. Then he said to me, 'Young man, there is a look in her eye that I don't like. There's something tricky about all her people. You watch yourself.'

He was right, of course. Dawn was cooking something up, and it wasn't chips.

When we got home we sat down over a nice cup of tea. She hadn't said a word during the whole drive.

I couldn't bear it any longer. I said, 'All right. What *is* the significance of that funny look.'

'I've decided we're going to get Mrs Chipperworth that divorce our client wants after all.'

'We are?'

'It's what we were hired to do, isn't it?'

I called Solicitor Goodrich to tell him that we had had success in our investigation and did he want our report.

He did. He was with us within twenty minutes.

I explained what I had seen the previous afternoon. I gave him the photographs I had taken of Chipperworth entering Mrs Elmitt's house with a key and, later, adjusting his flies as he came out. I reported what the neighbour had told me.

'She is willing to testify to what she's seen in court, or to swear out a statement,' I said. 'But she would like some money for it.'

'I think that can be arranged,' Goodrich said.

A little ready cash might help the old woman get some curtains for her own windows.

Goodrich wrote out a cheque for our fee and expenses on the spot.

'Of course, if *we* have to testify,' I said, 'there will be an additional bill.'

'I don't think it will come to that,' Goodrich said.

After he left I rang Rest Easy Beds.

I explained to Mr Chipperworth that we wanted to come over to speak to him.

'What is it that is so urgent, Mr Herring?' he said.

'We wanted to tell you about your wife's plans to sue you for divorce,' I said.

As soon as we arrived we were ushered into Chipperworth's office.

'But she's known about Madeleine for years,' he said when I explained what we'd been hired to do. 'It's an arrangement we have. She doesn't like *it*, you see. So Madeleine keeps me from making . . . demands.'

'She doesn't seem to mind the demands of her lover,' Dawn said.

'Her *what?*'

'Why don't you ask her about her telephone calls recently,' Dawn suggested. 'We have to be going now. Ta, ta.'

We stopped at Nigel's and then we went on home.

We didn't have long to wait.

A few minutes after noon the bell rang. Before I could get to it, pounding started on the door. When I opened it I faced Solicitor Goodrich, in a fury. He swung fists at me.

For the most part being as tall as I am is an inconvenience. But at least I have long arms and could keep him out of reach. When he finished flailing, he started swearing. The rude language seemed particularly unseemly for a member of the legal profession. I would have been very embarrassed for Dawn if I hadn't heard as bad or worse from her family. But they are foul-mouthed in a friendly way. Goodrich was vicious.

Also defamatory. He claimed that we had sold information to Mr Chipperworth.

I was about to deny it when Dawn said, 'What if we did?'

'I'll have you for this,' Goodrich said. 'It's illegal. I can put you in gaol.'

'That's fine talk from somebody who set fire to a warehouse.'

Goodrich was suddenly still and attentive. 'What?'

'You're the arsonist responsible for the fire at Rest Easy Beds.'

'That's silly talk,' Goodrich said. But he wasn't laughing.

'The idea was that when Mr Chipperworth collected the insurance money Mrs Chipperworth would start divorce proceedings which would entitle her to claim half of it. With your help she could probably settle out of court and between the insurance cash and her share of the rest of the joint property, you and Mrs Chipperworth would have a nice little nest egg to run away on.'

'Prove it,' Goodrich said.

'Oh, I think it's a very clever plan,' Dawn said charmingly. 'I suppose you have an alibi for the night of the fire?'

'Why should I need one?'

'Well, if we went to the police . . . '

'Why the hell should you do that?' Goodrich burst out.

'Ah,' Dawn said. 'Now we're getting down to the serious questions.' She batted her eyelashes. 'We never actually gave our evidence to Mr Chipperworth, you know, and as long as Mrs Chipperworth has denied everything . . . '

'You want money, I suppose,' Goodrich said.

'Well, poor Freddie is terribly tall, and a bigger car would be so much easier for him to get in and out of.'

'All right,' Goodrich said. 'A car.'

'And there are so many little improvements that ought to be made on this house.'

'How about just getting to a bottom-line figure.'

'I think thirty thousand would come in very handy, don't you Freddie?'

'Oh, very handy.'

'Thirty thousand!' Goodrich said.

'Yes,' Dawn said. 'See how reasonable we are?'

When the trial came along it was plastered all over the local papers. Frome is not so big a town that we get serious court cases involving local people every week.

Especially not cases involving solicitors and arson, not cases with a little titillation in them. Goodrich pleaded guilty, but the local reporter, Scoop Wall, tracked down Mrs Elmitt's neighbour who was photographed pointing to some of the uncurtained windows through which she had been forced to witness indescribable acts. Well, the descriptions didn't make the papers anyway.

Uncle Steve was not pleased at first when he heard what we had done.

Heard is the operative word because we had tape-recorded the entire conversation with Goodrich on equipment we borrowed from Cousin Nigel.

But Dawn explained. After all this time the only way Goodrich's arson would be proved was if he confessed to it. But the police couldn't have used the threat of exposing his relationship to Mrs Chipperworth the way we did because that would have transgressed legal niceties. 'So it was up to Freddie and me,' Dawn said.

Eventually Uncle Steve laughed.

'I warned you about her,' he said to me.

But it worked out all right in the end.

Except . . . Scoop Wall tracked down Dawn and me too.

We begged her not to put anything about us in the paper.

But she refused. We were key figures in bringing a dangerous solicitor to justice. It was news. And besides, Dawn has good legs and photographs well.

It's not that we weren't proud of what we – or let's be fair – what Dawn had done.

But it meant that the Frederick Herring Private Inquiry Agency burst from its quiet and planned total obscurity into the glare of public attention.

We started getting calls. We started getting visitors. We started getting letters. Find this, look for that, unravel the other.

And it wasn't actually the attention which was the problem.

The problem was that we found we quite liked it. See, some of the cases we were offered were pretty interesting. Rather like chess problems . . . So, we decided, maybe one more. Or two.

Something the Cat Dragged In

Patricia Highsmith

A few seconds of pondering silence in the scrabble game was
interrupted by a rustle of plastic at the cat door: Portland Bill
was coming in again. Nobody paid any attention. Michael and
Gladys Herbert were ahead. Gladys doing a bit better than her
husband. The Herberts played scrabble often and were quite
sharp at it. Colonel Edward Phelp – a neighbour and a good
friend – was limping along, and his American niece Phyllis, aged
nineteen, had been doing well but had lost interest in the last ten
minutes. It would soon be teatime. The Colonel was sleepy and
looked it.

'Quack,' said the Colonel thoughtfully, pushing a forefinger
against his Kipling-style moustache. 'Pity – was thinking of
earthquake.'

'If you've got *quack*, Uncle Eddie,' said Phyllis, 'how could you
get quake out of it?'

The cat made another more sustained noise at his door, and
now with black tail and brindle hindquarters in the house, he
moved backwards and pulled something through the plastic oval.
What he had dragged in looked whitish and about six inches
long.

'Caught another bird,' said Michael, impatient for Eddie to
take his turn so that he could make a brilliant move before
somebody grabbed it.

'Looks like another goose foot,' said Gladys, glancing. 'Ugh.'

The Colonel at last moved, adding a P to SUM. Michael
moved, raising a gasp of admiration from Phyllis for his INI
stuck on to GEM, followed in his next move by NATAL from
the N in GEMINI.

Portland Bill flipped his trophy into the air, and it fell on the
carpet with a thud.

'Really *dead* pigeon, that,' remarked the Colonel who was

16

nearest the cat, but whose eyesight was not of the best. 'Turnip,' he said for Phyllis's benefit. 'Swede. Or an oddly-shaped carrot,' he added, peering, then chuckled. 'I've seen carrots take the most fantastic shapes. Saw one once—'

'This is white,' added Phyllis, and got up to investigate, since Gladys had to play before her. In slacks and sweater, she bent over with hands on her knees. 'Good *Chr*—Oh! Uncle Eddie!' She stood up and clapped her hand over her mouth as if she had said something dreadful.

Michael Herbert had half-risen from his chair. 'What's the matter?'

'They're human *fingers*!' Phyllis said. 'Look!'

They all looked, coming slowly, unbelievingly, from the card table. The cat looked, proudly, up at the faces of the four humans gazing down. Gladys drew in her breath.

The two fingers were dead white and puffy, there was not a sign of blood even at the base of the fingers which included a couple of inches of what had been the hand. What made the object undeniably the third and fourth fingers of a human hand were the two nails, yellowish and short and looking small because of the swollen flesh.

'What should we do, Michael?' Gladys was practical, but liked to let her husband make decisions.

'That's been dead for two weeks at least,' murmured the Colonel, who had had some war experiences.

'Could it have come from a hospital near here?' asked Phyllis.

'Hospital amputating like that?' replied her uncle with a chuckle.

'The nearest hospital is twenty miles from here,' said Gladys.

'Mustn't let Edna see it.' Michael glanced at his watch. 'Of course I think we—'

'Maybe call the police?' asked Gladys.

'I was thinking of that. I—' Michael's hesitation was interrupted by Edna, their housekeeper-cook, bumping just then against a door in a remote corner of the big living-room. The tea tray had arrived. The others discreetly moved towards the low table in front of the fireplace, while Michael Herbert stood with an air of casualness. The fingers were just behind his shoes. Michael pulled an unlit pipe from his jacket pocket, and fiddled with it, blowing into its stem. His hands shook a little. He shooed Portland Bill away with one foot.

Edna finally dispensed napkins and plates, and said, 'Have a nice tea!' She was a local woman in her mid-fifties, a reliable soul, but with most of her mind on her own children and grandchildren – thank goodness, under these circumstances, Michael thought. Edna arrived at half-past seven in the morning on her bicycle and departed when she pleased, as long as there was something in the house for supper. The Herberts were not fussy.

Gladys was looking anxiously towards Michael. 'Get a–*way* Bill!'

'Got to do something with this meanwhile.' Michael murmured. With determination he went to the basket of newspapers beside the fireplace, shook out a page of *The Times*, and returned to the fingers which Portland Bill was about to pick up. Michael beat the cat by grabbing the fingers through the newspaper. The others had not sat down. Michael made a gesture for them to do so, and closed the newspaper around the fingers, rolling and folding. 'The thing to do, I should think,' said Michael, 'is to notify the police, because there might have been – foul play somewhere.'

'Or might it have fallen,' the Colonel began, shaking out his napkin, 'out of an ambulance or some disposal unit – you know? Might've been an accident somewhere.'

'Or should we just let well enough alone – and get rid of it?' said Gladys. 'I need some tea.' She had poured, and proceeded to sip her cup.

No one had an answer to her suggestion. It was as if the three others were stunned, or hypnotized by one another's presence, vaguely expecting a response from another which did not come.

'Rid of it where? In the garbage?' asked Phyllis. '*Bury* it,' she added, as if answering her own question.

'I don't think that would be right,' said Michael.

'Michael, do have some tea,' said his wife.

'Got to put this somewhere – overnight.' Michael still held the little bundle. 'Unless we ring the police now. It's already five and it's Sunday.'

'In England do the police care whether it's Sunday or not?' asked Phyllis.

Michael started for the cupboard near the front door, with an idea of putting the thing on top beside a couple of hat boxes, but he was followed by the cat, and Michael knew that with enough inspiration the cat could leap to the top.

'I've got just the thing, I think,' said the Colonel, pleased by his own idea, but with an air of calm in case Edna made a second appearance. 'Bought some houseslippers just yesterday in the High Street and I've still got the box. I'll go and fetch it, if I may.' He went off towards the stairs, then turned and said softly, 'We'll tie a string around it. Keep it away from the cat.' The Colonel climbed the stairs.

'Keep it in whose room?' asked Phyllis with a nervous giggle.

The Herberts did not answer. Michael, still on his feet, held the object in his right hand. Portland Bill sat with white forepaws neatly together, regarding Michael, waiting to see what Michael would do with it.

Colonel Phelps came down with his white cardboard shoe box. The little bundle went in easily, and Michael let the Colonel hold the box while he went to rinse his hands in the lavatory near the front door. When Michael returned, Portland Bill still hovered, and gave out a hopeful 'Miaow?'

'Let's put it in the sideboard cupboard for the moment,' said Michael, and took the box from Eddie's hands. He felt that the box at least was comparatively clean, and he put it beside a stack of large and seldom-used dinner plates, then closed the cabinet door which had a key in it.

Phyllis bit into a Bath Oliver and said, 'I noticed a crease in one finger. If there's a ring there, it might give a clue.'

Michael exchanged a glance with Eddie, who nodded slightly. They had both noticed the crease. Tacitly the men agreed to take care of this later.

'More tea, dear,' said Gladys. She refilled Phyllis's cup.

'M'wow,' said the cat in a disappointed tone. He was now seated facing the sideboard, looking over one shoulder.

Michael changed the subject: the progress of the Colonel's redecorating. The painting of the first-floor bedrooms was the main reason why the Colonel and his niece were visiting the Herberts just now. But this was of no interest compared to Phyllis's question to Michael:

'Shouldn't you ask if anyone's missing in the neighbourhood? Those fingers might be part of a *murder*.'

Gladys shook her head slightly and said nothing. Why did Americans always think in such violent terms? However, what could have severed a hand in such a manner? An explosion? An axe?

A lively scratching sound got Michael to his feet.

'Bill, do *stop* that!' Michael advanced on the cat and shooed him away. Bill had been trying to open the cabinet door.

Tea was over more quickly than usual. Michael stood by the sideboard while Edna cleared away.

'When're you going to look at the ring, Uncle Eddie?' Phyllis asked. She wore round-rimmed glasses and was rather myopic.

'I don't think Michael and I have quite decided what we should do, my dear,' said her uncle.

'Let's go into the library, Phyllis,' said Gladys. 'You said you wanted to look at some photographs.'

Phyllis had said that. There were photographs of Phyllis's mother and of the house where her mother had been born, in which Uncle Eddie now lived. Eddie was older than her mother by fifteen years. Now Phyllis wished she hadn't asked to see the photographs, because the men were going to do something with the *fingers*, and Phyllis would have liked to watch. After all, she was used to dissecting frogs and dogfish in zoology lab. But her mother had warned her before she left New York to mind her manners and not be 'crude and insensitive', her mother's usual adjectives about Americans. Phyllis dutifully sat looking at photographs fifteen and twenty years old, at least.

'Let's take it out to the garage,' Michael said to Eddie. 'I've got a workbench there, you know.'

The two men walked along a gravelled path to the two-car garage at the back of which Michael had a workshop with saws and hammers, chisels and electric drills, plus a supply of wood and planks in case the house needed any repairs or he felt in the mood to make something. Michael was a freelance journalist and book critic, but he enjoyed manual labour. Here he felt better with the awful box, somehow. He could set it on his sturdy workbench as if he were a surgeon laying out a body, or a corpse.

'What the hell do you make of this?' asked Michael as he flipped the fingers out by holding one side of the newspaper. The fingers flopped on to the well-used wooden surface, this time palm side upward. The white flesh was jagged where it had been cut, and in the strong beam of the spotlight which shone from over the bench, they could see two bits of metacarpals, also jagged, projecting from the flesh. Michael turned the fingers over with the tip of a screwdriver. He twisted the screwdriver tip, and parted the flesh enough to see the glint of gold.

'Gold ring,' said Eddie. 'But he was a workman of some kind, don't you think? Look at those nails. Short and thick. Still some soil under them – dirty, anyway.'

'I was thinking – if we report it to the police, shouldn't we leave it the way it is? Not try to look at the ring?'

'Are you going to report it to the police?' asked Eddie with a smile as he lit a small cigar. 'What'll you be in for then?'

'In for? I'll say the cat dragged it in. Why should I be in for anything – I'm curious about the ring. Might give us a clue.'

Colonel Phelps glanced at the garage door which Michael had closed but not locked. He too was curious about the ring. He was thinking, if it had been a gentleman's hand, they might have turned it in to the police by now. 'Many farm-workers around here still?' he mused. 'I suppose so.'

Michael shrugged, nervous. 'What do you say about the ring?'

'Let's have a look.' The Colonel puffed serenely, and looked at Michael's racks of tools.

'I know what we need.' Michael reached for a Stanley knife which he ordinarily used for cutting cardboard, pushed the blade out with his thumb, and placed his fingers on the pudgy remainder of the palm. He made a cut above where the ring was, then below.

Eddie Phelps bent to watch. 'No blood at all. Drained out. Just like the war days.'

Nothing but a goose foot, Michael was telling himself in order not to faint. Michael repeated his cuts on the top surface of the finger. He felt like asking Eddie if he wanted to finish the job, but he thought that might be cowardly.

'Dear me,' Eddie murmured unhelpfully.

Michael had to cut off some strips of flesh, then take a firm grip with both hands to get the wedding ring off. It most certainly was a wedding ring of plain gold, not very thick or broad, but suitable for a man to wear. Michael rinsed it at the cold water tap of the sink on his left. When he held it near the spotlight, initials were legible: *W.R–M.T.*

Eddie peered. 'Now that's a clue!'

Michael heard the cat scratching at the garage door, then a miaow. Next Michael put the three pieces of flesh he had cut off into an old rag, wadded it up, and told Eddie he would be back in a minute. He opened the garage door, discouraged Bill with a '*Whisht!*' and stuck the rag into a dustbin which had a fastening that a cat could not open. Michael had thought he had a plan to propose to Eddie, but when he returned – Eddie was again examining the ring – he was too shaken to speak. He had meant to say something about making 'discreet inquiries'. Instead he said in a voice gone hollow:

'Let's call it a day – unless we think of something brilliant tonight. Let's leave the box here. The cat can't get in.'

Michael didn't want to leave the box even on his workbench. He put the ring in with the fingers, and set the box atop some plastic jerricans which stood against a wall. His workshop was even ratproof, so far. Nothing was going to come in to chew at the box.

As Michael got into bed that night, Gladys said, 'If we don't tell the police, we've simply got to bury it somewhere.'

'Yes,' said Michael vaguely. It seemed somehow a criminal act, burying a pair of human fingers. He had told Gladys about the ring. The initials hadn't rung any bell with her.

Colonel Edward Phelps went to sleep quite peacefully, having reminded himself that he had seen a lot worse in 1941.

Phyllis had quizzed her uncle and Michael about the ring at dinner. Maybe it would all be solved tomorrow and turn out to be – somehow – something quite simple and innocent. Anyway, it would make quite a story to tell her chums in college. And her mother! So this was the quiet English countryside!

The next day being Monday, with the post office open, Michael decided to pose a question to Mary Jeffrey who doubled as postal clerk and grocery salesgirl in the establishment. Michael bought some stamps, then asked casually:

'By the way, Mary, is anybody missing lately – in this neighbourhood?'

Mary, a bright-faced girl with dark curly hair, looked puzzled. 'Missing how?'

'Disappeared.' Michael said with a smile.

Mary shook her head. 'Not that I know about. Why do you ask?'

Michael had tried to prepare for this. 'I read somewhere in a newspaper that people do sometimes – just disappear, even in small villages like this. Drift away, change their names or some such. Baffles everyone, where they go.' Michael was drifting away himself. Not a good job, but the question was put.

He walked the quarter of a mile back home, wishing he had had the guts to ask Mary if anyone in the area had a bandaged left hand, or if she'd heard of any such accident. Mary had boy-friends who frequented the local pub. Mary this minute might know of a man with a bandaged hand, but Michael could not possibly tell her that the missing fingers were in his garage.

The matter of what to do with the fingers was put aside for that morning, as the Herberts had laid on a drive to Cambridge, followed by lunch at the house of a don who was a friend of theirs. Unthinkable to cancel that because of getting involved with the police, so the fingers did not come up in conversation that morning. They talked of anything else during the drive. Michael and Gladys and Eddie had decided, before taking off for Cambridge, that they should not discuss the fingers again in front of Phyllis, but let it blow over, if possible. Eddie and Phyllis were to leave on the afternoon of Wednesday, the day after tomorrow, and by then the matter might be cleared up or in the hands of the police.

Gladys had also gently warned Phyllis not to bring up 'the cat incident' at the don's house, so Phyllis did not. All went well and happily, and the Herberts and Eddie and Phyllis were back at the Herbert's house around four. Edna told Gladys she had just realized they were short of butter, and since she was watching a cake – Michael, in the living-room with Eddie, heard this and volunteered to go to the grocery.

Michael bought the butter, a couple of packets of cigarettes, a box of toffee that looked nice, and was served by Mary in her usual modest and polite manner. He had been hoping for news from her. Michael had taken his change and was walking to the door, when Mary cried: 'Oh, Mr Herbert!'

Michael turned round.

'I heard of someone disappearing just this noon,' Mary said, leaning towards Michael across the counter, smiling now. 'Bill Reeves – lives on Mr Dickensons's property, you know. He has a cottage there, works on the land – or did.'

Michael didn't know Bill Reeves, but he certainly knew of the Dickenson property, which was vast, to the northwest of the village. Bill Reeve's initials fitted with the W.R. on the ring. 'Yes? He disappeared?'

'About two weeks ago. Mr Vickers told me. Mr Vickers has the petrol station near the Dickenson property, you know. He came in today, so I thought I'd ask him.' She smiled again, as if she had done satisfactorily with Michael's little riddle.

Michael knew the petrol station and knew how Vickers looked, vaguely. 'Interesting. Does Mr Vickers know why he disappeared?'

'No. He said it's a mystery. Bill Reeves's wife left the cottage too, a few days ago, but everyone knows she went to Manchester to stay with her sister there.'

Michael nodded. 'Well, well. Shows it can happen even here, eh? People disappearing.' He smiled and went out of the post office-grocery.

The thing to do was ring up Tom Dickenson, Michael thought, and ask him what he knew. Michael didn't call him Tom, had met him only a couple of times at local political rallies and such. Dickenson was about thirty, married, had inherited, and now led the life of gentleman farmer, Michael thought. The family was in the wool industry, had factories up north, and had owned their land here for generations.

When he got home, Michael had asked Eddie to come up to his study, and despite Phyllis's curiosity, did not invite her to join them. Michael told Eddie what Mary had said about the disappearance of a farm-worker called Bill Reeves a couple of weeks ago. Eddie agreed that they might ring up Dickenson.

'The initials on the ring could be an accident,' Eddie said. 'The Dickenson place is fifteen miles from here, you say.'

'Yes, but I still think I'll ring him.' Michael looked up the number in the directory on his desk. There were two numbers. Michael tried the first.

A servant, or someone who sounded like a servant, answered, inquired Michael's name, then said he would summon Mr Dickenson. Michael waited a good minute. Eddie was waiting too. 'Hello, Mr Dickenson. I'm one of your neighbours, Michael Herbert . . . Yes, yes, I know we have – couple of times. Look I have a question to ask which you might think odd, but – I understand you had a workman or tenant on your land called Bill Reeves?'

'Ye—es?' replied Tom Dickenson.

'And where is he now – I'm asking because I was told he disappeared a couple of weeks ago.'

'Yes, that's true. Why do you ask?'

'Do you know where he went?'

'No idea,' replied Dickenson. 'Did you have any dealings with him?'

'No. Could you tell me what his wife's name is?'

'Marjorie.'

That fitted the first initial. 'Do you happen to know her maiden name?'

Tom Dickenson chuckled. 'I'm afraid I don't.'

Michael glanced at Eddie, who was watching him. 'Do you know if Bill Reeves wore a wedding ring?'

'No. Never paid that much attention to him. Why?'

Why, indeed? Michael shifted. If he ended the conversation here, he would not have learned much. 'Because—I've found something that just might be a clue in regard to Bill Reeves. I presume someone's looking for him, if no one knows his whereabouts.'

'I'm not looking for him,' Tom Dickenson replied in his easy manner. 'I doubt if his wife is, either. She moved out a week ago. May I ask what you found?'

'I'd rather not say over the telephone. I wonder if I could come to see you. Or perhaps you could come to my house.'

After an instant of silence, Dickenson said, 'Quite honestly, I'm not interested in Reeves. I don't think he left any debts, as far as I know, I'll say that for him. But I don't care what's happened to him, if I may speak frankly.'

'I see. Sorry to've bothered you, Mr Dickenson.'

They hung up.

Michael turned to Eddie Phelps and said, 'I think you got most of that. Dickenson's not interested.'

'Can't expect Dickenson to be concerned about the dis-appeared farm-worker. Did I hear him say the wife's gone too?'

'Thought I told you. She went to Manchester to her sister's, Mary told me.' Michael took a pipe from the rack on his desk and began to fill it. 'Wife's name is Marjorie. Fits the initial on the ring.'

'True,' said the Colonel, 'but there're lots of Marys and Margarets in the world.'

'Dickenson didn't know her maiden name. Now look, Eddie, with no help from Dickenson, I'm thinking we ought to buzz the police and get this over with. I'm sure I can't bring myself to bury that – object – even in the woods adjacent which don't belong to anybody. The thing would haunt me. I'd be thinking a dog would dig it up, even if it's just bones or in a *worse* state, and the police would have to start with somebody else besides me, and with a trail not so fresh to follow.'

'You're still thinking of foul play? – I have a simpler idea,' Eddie said with an air of calm and logic. 'Gladys said there was a hospital twenty miles away, I presume in Colchester. We might ask if in the last two weeks or so there's been an accident involving the loss of third and fourth fingers of a man's left hand. They'd have his name. It looks like an accident and of the kind that doesn't happen every day.'

Michael was on the brink of agreeing to this, at least before ringing the police, when the telephone rang. Michael took it, and found Gladys on the line downstairs with a man whose voice sounded like Dickenson's. 'I'll take it, Gladys.'

Tom Dickenson said hello to Michael. 'I've – I thought if you really would like to see me—'

'I'd be very glad to.'

'I'd prefer to speak with you alone, if that's possible.'

Michael assured him it was, and Dickenson said he could come along in about twenty minutes. Michael put the telephone down with a feeling of relief, and said to Eddie, 'He's coming over now and wants to talk with me alone. That *is* the best.'

'Yes.' Eddie got up from Michael's sofa, disappointed. 'He'll be more open, if he has anything to say. Are you going to tell him about the fingers?' He peered at Michael sideways, bushy eyebrows raised.

'May not come to that. I'll see what he has to say first.'

'He's going to ask you what you found.'

Michael knew that. They went downstairs. Michael saw Phyllis in the back garden, banging a croquet ball all by herself, and heard Gladys's voice in the kitchen. Michael informed Gladys, out of Edna's hearing, of the imminent arrival of Tom Dickenson, and explained why: Mary's information that a certain Bill Reeves was missing, a worker on Dickenson's property. Gladys realized at once that the initial matched.

And here came Dickenson's car, a black Triumph convertible,

rather in need of a wash. Michael went out to greet him. Hellos, and you remember mes. They vaguely remembered each other. Michael invited Dickenson into the house before Phyllis could drift over and compel an introduction.

Tom Dickenson was blond and tallish, now in leather jacket and corduroys and green rubber boots which he assured Michael were not muddy. He had just been working on his land, and hadn't taken the time to change.

'Let's go up,' said Michael, leading the way to the stairs.

Michael offered Dickenson a comfortable armchair, and sat down on his old sofa. 'You told me – Bill Reeves's wife went off too?'

Dickenson smiled a little, and his bluish-grey eyes gazed calmly at Michael. 'His wife left, yes. But that was after Reeves vanished. Majorie went to Manchester, I heard. She has a sister there. The Reeveses weren't getting on so well. They're both about twenty-five – Reeves fond of his drink. I'll be glad to replace him, frankly. Easily done.'

Michael waited for more. It didn't come. Michael was wondering why Dickenson had been willing to come to see him about a farm-worker he didn't much like?

'Why're you interested?' Dickenson asked. Then he broke out in a laugh which made him look younger and happier. 'Is Reeves perhaps asking for a job with you – under another name?'

'Not at all.' Michael smiled too. 'I haven't anywhere to lodge a worker. No.'

'But you said you found something?' Tom Dickenson's brows drew in a polite frown of inquiry.

Michael looked at the floor, then lifted his eyes and said, 'I found two fingers of a man's left hand – with a wedding ring on one finger. The initials on the ring could stand for William Reeves. The other initials are M.T., which could be Marjorie somebody. That's why I thought I should ring you up.'

Had Dickenson's face gone paler, or was Michael imagining? Dickenson's lips were slightly parted, his eyes uncertain. 'Good Lord, found it where?'

'Our cat dragged it in—believe it or not. Had to tell my wife, because the cat brought it into the living-room in front of all of us.' Somehow it was a tremendous relief for Michael to get the words out. 'My old friend Eddie Phelps and his American niece are here now. They saw it.' Michael stood up. Now he wanted a cigarette, got the box from his desk and offered it to Dickenson.

Dickenson said he had just stopped smoking, but he would like one.

'It was a bit shocking,' Michael went on, 'so I thought I'd make some inquiries in the neighbourhood before I spoke to the police. I think informing the police is the right thing to do. Don't you?'

Dickenson did not answer at once.

'I had to cut away some of the finger to get the ring off – with Eddie's assistance last night.' Dickenson still said nothing, only drew on his cigarette, frowning. 'I thought the ring might give a clue, which it does, though it might have nothing at all to do with Bill Reeves. You don't seem to know if he wore a wedding ring, and you don't know Marjorie's maiden name.'

'Oh, that one can find out.' Dickenson's voice sounded different and more husky.

'Do you think we should do that? Or maybe you know where Reeves's parents live? Or Marjorie's parents? Maybe Reeves is at one or the other's place now.'

'Not at his wife's parents', I'll bet,' said Dickenson with a nervous smile. 'She's fed up with him.'

'Well – what do you think? I'll tell the police? Would you like to see the ring?'

'No, I'll take your word.'

'Then I'll get in touch with the police tomorrow – or this evening. I suppose the sooner the better.' Michael noticed Dickenson glancing around the room as if he might see the fingers lying on a bookshelf.

The study door moved and Portland Bill walked in. Michael never quite closed his door, and Bill had an assured way with doors, rearing a little and giving them a push.

Dickenson blinked at the cat, then said to Michael in a firm voice, 'I could stand a scotch. May I?'

Michael went downstairs and brought back the bottle and two glasses in his hands. There had been no one in the living-room. Michael poured. Then he shut the door of his study.

Dickenson took a good inch of his drink at the first gulp. 'I may as well tell you now that I killed Reeves.'

A tremor went over Michael's shoulders, yet he told himself that he had known this all along – or since Dickenson's telephone call to him, anyway. 'Yes?' said Michael.

'Reeves had been – trying it on with my wife. I won't give it the dignity of calling it an affair. I blame my wife – flirting in a silly way with Reeves. He was just a lout, as far as I'm concerned. Handsome and stupid. His wife knew, and she hated him for it. 'Dickenson drew on the last of his cigarette, and Michael fetched the box again. Dickenson took one. 'Reeves got ever more sure of himself. I wanted to sack him and send him away, but I couldn't because of his lease on the cottage, and I didn't want to bring the situation with my wife to light – with the law, I mean – as a reason.'

'How long did this go on?'

Dickenson had to think. 'Maybe about a month.'

'And your wife—now?'

Tom Dickenson sighed, and rubbed his eyes. He sat hunched forward in his chair. 'We'll patch it up. We've hardly been married a year.'

'She knows you killed Reeves?'

Now Dickenson sat back, propped a green boot on one knee, and drummed the fingers of one hand on the arm of his chair. 'I don't know. She may think I just sent him packing. She didn't ask any questions.'

Michael could imagine, and he could also see that Dickenson would prefer that his wife never knew. Michael realized that he would have to make a decision: to turn Dickenson over to the police or not. Or would Dickenson even prefer to be turned in? Michael was listening to the confession of a man who had had a crime on his conscience for more than two weeks, bottled up inside himself, or so Michael assumed. And how had

Dickenson killed him? 'Does anyone else know?' Michael asked cautiously.

'Well – I can tell you about that. I suppose I must. Yes.' Dickenson's voice was again hoarse, and his whisky gone.

Michael got up and replenished Dickenson's glass.

Dickenson sipped now, and stared at the wall beside Michael.

Portland Bill sat at a little distance from Michael, concentrating on Dickenson as if he understood every word and was waiting for the next instalment.

'I told Reeves to stop playing about with my wife or leave my property with his own wife, but he brought up the lease—and why didn't I speak to *my* wife. Arrogant, you know, so pleased with himself that the master's wife had deigned to look at him and—' Dickenson began again. 'Tuesdays and Fridays I go to London to take care of the company. A couple of times, Diane said she didn't feel like going to London or she had some other engagement. Reeves could always manage a little work close to the house on those days, I'm sure. And then – there was a second victim – like me.'

'Victim? What do you mean?'

'Peter.' Now Dickenson rolled his glass between his hands, the cigarette projected from his lips, and he stared at the wall beside Michael, and spoke as if he were narrating what he saw on a screen there. 'We were trimming some hedgerows deep in the fields, cutting stakes too for new markings. Reeves and I. Axes and sledgehammers. Peter was driving in stakes quite a way from us. Peter's another hand like Reeves, been with me longer. I had the feeling Reeves might attack me – then say it was an accident or some such. It was afternoon, and he'd had a few pints at lunch. He had a hatchet. I didn't turn my back on him, and my anger was somehow rising. He had a smirk on his face, and he swung his hatchet as if to catch me in the thigh, though he wasn't near enough to me. Then he turned his back on me – arrogantly – and I hit him in the head with the big hammer. I hit him a second time as he was falling, but that landed on his back. I didn't know Peter was so close to me, or I

didn't think about that. Peter came running, with his axe. Peter said, "Good! Damn the bastard!" or something like that, and—'
Dickenson seemed stuck for words, and looked at the floor, then the cat.

'And then? Reeves was dead?'

'Yes. All this happened in seconds. Peter really finished it with a bash on Reeves's head with the axe. We were quite near some woods – my woods. Peter said, "Let's bury the swine! Get rid of him!" Peter was in a cursing rage and I was out of my mind for a different reason, maybe shock, but Peter was saying that Reeves had been having it off with his wife too, or trying to, and that he knew about Reeves and Diane. Peter and I dug a grave in the woods, both of us working like madmen – hacking at tree roots and throwing up earth with our hands. At the last, just before we threw him in, Peter took the hatchet and said – something about Reeves's wedding ring, and he brought the hatchet down a couple of times on Reeves's hand.'

Michael did not feel so well. He leaned over, mainly to lower his head, and stroked the cat's strong back. The cat still concentrated on Dickenson.

'Then – we buried it, both of us drenched in sweat by then. Peter said, "You won't get a word out of me, sir. This bastard deserved what he got." We trampled the grave and Peter spat on it. Peter's a man, I'll say that for him.'

'A man. And you?'

'I dunno.' Dickenson's eyes were serious when he next spoke. 'That was one of the days Diane had a tea date at some women's club in our village. The same afternoon I thought, my God, the fingers! Maybe they're just lying there on the ground, because I couldn't remember Peter or myself throwing them into the grave. So I went back. I found them. I could've dug another hole, except that I hadn't brought anything to dig with and I also didn't want – anything more of Reeves on my land. So I got into my car and drove, not caring where, not paying any attention to where I was, and when I saw some woods, I got out and flung the thing as far as I could.'

Michael said, 'Must've been within half a mile of this house.

Portland Bill doesn't venture farther, I think. He's been doctored, poor old Bill.' The cat looked up at his name. 'You trust this Peter?'

'I do, I knew his father and so did my father. And if I were asked – I'm not sure I could say who struck the fatal blow, Peter or I. But to be correct, *I'd* take the responsibility, because I did strike two blows with the hammer. I can't claim self-defence, because Reeves hadn't attacked me.'

Correct. An odd word, Michael thought. But Dickenson was the type who would want to be correct. 'What do you propose to do now?'

'Propose? I?' Dickenson's sigh was almost a gasp. 'I dunno. I've admitted it. In a way it's in your hands or—' He made a gesture to indicate the downstairs. 'I'd like to spare Peter – keep him out of it – if I can. You understand, I think. I can talk to you. You're a man like myself.'

Michael was not sure of that, but he had been trying to imagine himself in Dickenson's position, trying to see himself twenty years younger in the same circumstances. Reeves had been a swine – even to his own wife – unprincipled, and should a young man like Dickenson ruin his own life, or the best part of it, over a man like Reeves? 'What about Reeves's wife?'

Dickenson shook his head and frowned, 'I know she detested him. If he's absent without tidings, I'll wager she'll never make the least effort to find him. She's glad to be rid of him, I'm sure.'

A silence began and grew. Portland Bill yawned, arched his back and stretched. Dickenson watched the cat as if he might say something: after all the cat had discovered the fingers. But the cat said nothing. Dickenson broke the silence awkwardly but in a polite tone:

'Where are the fingers—by the way?'

'In the back of my garage – which is locked. They're in a shoe box.' Michael felt quite off balance. 'Look, I have two guests in the house.'

Tom Dickenson got to his feet quickly. 'I know. Sorry.'

'Nothing to be sorry about, but I've really got to *say* something to them because the Colonel – my old friend Eddie – knows I

33

rang you up about the initials on the ring and that you were to call on us – me. He could've said something to the others.'

'Of course. I understand.'

'Could you stay here for a few minutes while I speak with the people downstairs? Feel free with the whisky.'

'Thank you.' His eyes did not flinch.

Michael went downstairs. Phyllis was kneeling by the gramophone, about to put a record on. Eddie Phelps sat in a corner of the sofa reading a newspaper. 'Where's Gladys?' Michael asked.

Gladys was deadheading roses. Michael called to her. She wore rubber boots like Dickenson, but hers were smaller and bright red. Michael looked to see if Edna was behind the kitchen door. Gladys said Edna had gone off to buy something at the grocery. Michael told Dickenson's story, trying to make it brief and clear. Phyllis's mouth fell open a couple of times. Eddie Phelps held his chin in a wise-looking fashion and said, 'Um-hm' now and then.

'I really don't feel like turning him in – or even speaking to the police.' Michael ventured in a voice hardly above a whisper. No one had said anything after his narration, and he had waited several seconds. 'I don't see why we can't just let it blow over. What's the harm?'

'What's the harm, yes,' said Eddie Phelps, but it might have been a mindless echo for all the help it gave Michael.

'I've heard of stories like this – among primitive peoples,' said Phyllis earnestly, as if to say she found Tom Dickenson's action quite justifiable.

Michael had of course included the resident worker Peter in his account. Had Dickenson's hammer blow been fatal, or the blow of Peter's axe? 'The primitive ethic is not what I'm concerned with,' Michael said, and at once felt confused. In regard to Tom Dickenson he was concerned with just the opposite of the primitive.

'But what else is it?' asked Phyllis.

'Yes, yes,' said the Colonel, gazing at the ceiling.

'Really, Eddie,' said Michael, 'you're not being much of a help.'

'I'd say nothing about it. Bury those fingers somewhere – with the ring. Or maybe the ring in a different place for safety. Yes.' The Colonel was almost muttering, murmuring, but he did look at Michael.

'I'm not sure,' said Gladys, frowning with thought.

'I agree with Uncle Eddie,' Phyllis said, aware that Dickenson was upstairs awaiting his verdict. 'Mr Dickenson was provoked – *seriously* – and the man who got killed seems to have been a creep!'

'That's not the way the law looks at it,' Michael said with a wry smile. 'Lots of people are provoked seriously. And a human life is a human life.'

'*We're* not the law,' said Phyllis, as if they were something superior to the law just then.

Michael had been thinking just that: they were not the law, but they were acting as if they were. He was inclined to go along with Phyllis – and Eddie. 'All right. I don't feel like reporting this, given all the circumstances—'

But Gladys held out. She wasn't sure. Michael knew his wife well enough to believe that it was not going to be a bone of contention between them, if they were at variance—just now. So Michael said, 'You're one against three, Glad. Do you seriously want to ruin a young man's life for a thing like this?'

'True, we've got to take a vote, as if we were a jury,' said Eddie.

Gladys saw the point. She conceded. Less than a minute later, Michael climbed the stairs to his study, where the first draft of a book review curled in the roller of his typewriter, untouched since the day before yesterday. Fortunately he could still meet the deadline without killing himself.

'We don't want to report this to the police,' Michael said.

Dickenson, on his feet, nodded solemnly as if receiving a verdict. He would have nodded in the same manner if he had been told the opposite Michael thought.

'I'll get rid of the fingers,' Michael mumbled, and bent to get some pipe tobacco.

'Surely that's my responsibility. Let me bury them somewhere – with the ring.'

It really was Dickenson's responsibility, and Michael was glad to escape the task. 'Right. Well – shall we go downstairs? Would you like to meet my wife and my friend Colonel—'

'No, thank you. Not just now,' Dickenson interrupted. 'Another time. But would you give them – my thanks?'

They went down some other stairs at the back of the hall, and out to the garage, for which Michael had the key in his key case. He thought for a moment that the shoe box might have disappeared mysteriously as in a detective story, but it was exactly where he had left it, atop the oil jerricans. He gave it to Dickenson, and Dickenson departed northward in his dusty Triumph. Michael entered his house by the front door.

By now the others were having a drink. Michael felt suddenly relieved, and he smiled. 'I think old Portland ought to have something special at the cocktail hour, don't you?' Michael said, mainly to Gladys.

Portland Bill was looking without much interest at a bowl of ice cubes. Only Phyllis said '*Yes*' with enthusiasm.

Michael went to the kitchen and spoke with Edna who was dusting flour onto a board. 'Any more smoked salmon left from lunch?'

'One slice, sir,' said Edna, as if it weren't worth serving to anyone, and she virtuously hadn't eaten it, though she might.

'Can I have it for old Bill? He adores it.' When Michael came back into the living-room with the pink slice on a saucer, Phyllis said:

'I bet Mr Dickenson wrecks his car on the way home. That's often the way it is.' She whispered suddenly, remembering her manners. 'Because he feels *guilty*.'

Portland Bill bolted his salmon with brief but intense delight.

Tom Dickenson did not wreck his car.

Superfluous Murder

Milward Kennedy

As the train came to a standstill and he alighted from his carriage, John Mansbridge was amazed at the steadiness of his nerves. It was long since he had felt so calm and serene. Perhaps it was because he had reached a definite decision, after weeks of agonized doubt and fear. And yet his decision was not absolutely definite. He did not intend his visit to end in his cousin's murder if there was any hitch, however slight, in his careful yet simple plan.

In accordance with the plan, he engaged the ticket-collector in conversation about a mythical parcel which he pretended to have left on the platform on the occasion of his last visit, nearly a month ago. Naturally, he could get no news of it, but time enough was occupied to make him leave the station a clear five minutes after the few other passengers who had left the train at Gorse Hill had departed into the night.

'By Jove!' he said to the ticket-collector, looking up at the station clock, 'is it as late as that? My cousin, Mr Felix Mansbridge, will be wondering what has become of me, and it will take me a good three-quarters of an hour to walk to his house.'

'All of that, sir, on a night like this,' said the ticket-collector, and bade him a good night which was the more cordial for the shilling which was slipped into his hand.

John Mansbridge stepped briskly out of the station and down the country road towards the village. So far, so good. he had clearly established two facts: to wit, the time when he had left the station, and his intention to make his way on foot to his cousin's house.

He walked rapidly to the village and stopped at the *Four Feathers* to repeat his inquiry about his parcel—there was just a chance, he suggested, that he had left it there. Again he was at pains to establish the time of his visit; it was just on closing time, so he made his drink a short one. To himself he reflected that the whisky would put just the right edge on his judgment.

Then he went on his way, and at the far end of the village called a cheerful good night to the policeman on duty there. He smiled in the darkness to reflect that the police system was an integral part of his plan. In something under an hour's time the constable would be relieved, and his relief came down the lonely hill past Felix's house.

He walked on steadily, treading rather heavily to ensure that the policeman heard him, until he had turned the next corner. Then he took to his heels along the grass at the edge of the road, climbed a gate on the left, and doubled along a cart-track which led back to the other side of the village. He did not follow it to its end, but turned off across a smooth meadow and found his way without difficulty to a tumble-down shed. He pulled the door open and, drawing an electric torch from his pocket, flashed it on the interior before entering. He gave an involuntary sigh of satisfaction – the dust was undisturbed since his last visit; it seemed safe to assume that the presence of the bicycle had not been noticed.

He had taken great pains with that bicycle – bought it second-hand, and yet in good condition, with tyres well worn (so that they left no distinctive tracks) and yet with plenty of life in them. The dealer in the far-away Gloucestershire town who had sold it to him had taken no particular interest in the deal, and its transport to Gorse Hill had been effected by slow and unobtrusive stages – the last of them, to the abandoned shed, under the cover of darkness. The heap of loose sand inside the shed afforded an admirable means of covering up all signs of the use to which its shelter had been put.

He repeated his precautions, steeling himself against a tendency to hustle. The bicycle was carefully lifted out of the shed and leant against the wall; the heap of sand was used to conceal the marks of his feet; the heap itself was artistically arranged. Then he carried the bicycle to the footpath beyond the shed and mounted it.

Dark as the night was, he found it easy to follow the track.

Thanks to the drought, it was hard and firm and he made good speed. Not only that, he was confident that there would be few, if any, traces of his passage. The wind at his back also helped him on his course.

Nor did he hear or see a soul; the dogs, even, at the one farmhouse which he passed at some distance on his right, failed, apparently, to detect him. Almost before he realized it, a dark shimmer told him he had reached his first objective, the pond. He dismounted and, wheeling the bicycle, made his way cautiously to the spot which he had previously marked down as suitable to his purpose – where the bank was covered with short, dry stubble and where, he knew, the water was nearly four feet deep up to the very edge.

He knelt and lowered the bicycle silently into the pond. It was a little more difficult than he had expected, but still, his plan worked smoothly. The bicycle certainly had disappeared; it would be invisible in the dirty water and soon would sink into the soft mud and slime. So far as he could judge, the surface weeds would not look as though they had been wilfully and rather drastically disturbed. Deliberately he did what he could to improve this impression.

But he could not afford to linger; on the second stage of his journey time was of vital importance. He left the footpath, skirted the far end of the pond, climbed another gate, and ran across the field beyond it. From the far side he came in sight of his cousin's house. A soft light shone from the windows of the study, but otherwise there was no sign of life. That was as it should be; the married couple who 'did' for Felix were away on holiday and he was being ministered to by a woman from the village who 'came in by the day.'

John Mansbridge hurried on till he reached the gate at the bottom of the garden. Here he forced himself to pause in order to recover his breath. His heart was pounding against his ribs – this he firmly ascribed to his physical efforts and not to excitement.

Very cautiously he pulled out his watch and flashed his torch in its face. Again he sighed, this time not so much in contentment as because Fate seemed to have committed him to the deed. He had 'gained' a good twenty minutes – in other words, he had reached the house some twenty-two minutes before, on the evidence which he had created, it was possible for him to have done so. He was satisfied that he had arrived in entire secrecy, and it had taken him two minutes less than he had allowed.

He opened the gate and closed it behind him so carefully that the latch did not make a sound. He walked swiftly up the path – or rather the grass border – until he came to the lawn. He tiptoed across it towards the windows. They were closed, and the thin red curtains drawn. He leant close to the glass, though careful not to touch it, and with a shock detected the sound of a voice which seemed strange to him. Had all his plan split upon a single rock?

He crept round to the window at the other side. It was open, and though this side was sheltered from the breeze, the curtain had blown sufficiently aside to give him a clear view of most of the room. Simultaneously his lips smiled and his heart gave a fierce thump. The 'strange voice' was that of the loudspeaker, delivering a lecture on Babylonian pottery. Apparently it had had the effect of sending Felix to sleep.

He was sitting in an arm-chair of the 'grandmother' variety; its back was towards the door, so that it was sideways to the window through which John Mansbridge was peering. His bald head was lodged comfortably on a cushion, and his eyes were closed. His thin hands clasped the arms of the chair. He looked ill and tired, and his cousin felt almost sorry for him, till he noticed also the smug little smile on his lips. On the table beside him were a tumbler and a reading-lamp and a paper or two. On a table in the middle of the room stood a tray containing a small whisky decanter, a siphon, and a couple more glasses.

Anger welled up in John Mansbridge. How infernally comfortable and smug Felix was! Always so full of advice and patronage, and at the same time as mean as sin.

All very well to 'advise you, my dear John, to settle down to a steady job; give up the night club and melodrama existence.' As if he didn't know perfectly well that if Felix wasn't so infernally afraid of hurting himself and that heart which he pretended was so weak (as a matter of fact, he probably hadn't got such a thing), he'd have been painting the world red himself. Except that he was so mean. Positively hurt him to spend a halfpenny. Always whining about having no money. Damn it, hadn't he, John, seen the old man's will. He knew damned well that Felix had inherited a fat fortune. And when his only living relative asked him for a hundred or two, to help things along, he said he couldn't do it. Paying off debts of his father's.

Damned lie, that's what it was. Enough to make any one – well – sign the wrong name on a cheque. It ought to teach Felix a lesson, but the chances were that it would lead him to suppose that a lecture on morality was called for. All very fine to be honest when you've got more money than you want, and hate spending any of it. Canting hypocrite, that's all Felix was; piously swearing he was a poor man. 'All I can do, John, is to carry a large insurance on my life. And I had to pay a stiff price for that – it was all I could do to get the company to accept me at all. My heart, you know. Still, I wanted to do what I could for you, and I'm not likely to live long.'

No, he was not likely to live long, but it wouldn't be his heart that finished him off. And when he wrote that note asking his cousin to come and see him one day next week about a 'cheque which he didn't quite understand,' he finally settled his own fate. If the shock of what his cousin said didn't polish him off then and there (which wasn't likely; nothing wrong with his heart at all), then something else would. And John Mansbridge felt almost grateful to his cousin for being so feeble and flabby; he wouldn't put up much of a fight even for his life.

These thoughts, of a kind which had haunted him for weeks, flashed through John Mansbridge's mind in the second or two which he spent at the window. They served to give him fresh strength and determination.

A new thought suddenly struck him. There was Felix, to all appearances fast asleep. If he crept in noiselessly enough, he might be able to finish him off there, in the chair. It would be easy to fake signs of a struggle afterwards. That Indian club hanging in the hall. But suppose Felix woke up and saw him? Well, it would only curtail the interview. True, he would be sorry not to fire off the speech he had rehearsed, but that was a small point. Damn it, he'd have a shot at it.

He crouched on the lawn and cautiously took off his shoes; he tied the laces together for ease of carrying. He slipped on the gloves which were in his pocket and drew out from his ticket-pocket the 'spare' latch-key which he had so successfully purloined when last he was down at Gorse Hill. He crept round to the front door, deposited his shoes on the doorstep and, with infinite precaution, slipped the key into the Yale lock. To his satisfaction the door opened silently. He dared not turn on the hall light, but there was sufficient illumination from the half-open door of the study to show him all that he needed to see.

There was a faint scrape as he withdrew the key. He paused, but no sound came from the study. A second later the front door was safely and securely closed again. He took down an Indian club (not the first, but the one by the door of the dining-room), and tried its weight with a savage grin. Slipping the door-key back into his pocket, he advanced silently into the study.

Felix had not stirred - a nice way to welcome your only cousin! There was his bald head temptingly visible above the back of the chair. John stepped forward and swung the club. . .

That was that. All old scores wiped out. No need to make sure of the result – and no need to look at it. One had done things of the same kind in the war and felt none the worse. Funny what a difference there was, all the same. Still, no time to lose. No use getting sentimental. Find the cheque, that was the first thing. That ought not to be difficult – Felix would be sure to have it at hand, all ready for the interview; probably in the top drawer of the writing-desk. He jumped as he suddenly became conscious that the voice of the Babylonian expert filled the room, and with an oath he switched off the wireless. Now for the cheque.

But there was no forged cheque in the top drawer, and none in any other drawer of the desk. He began to tear envelopes open feverishly; pulled open the cupboard below the bookshelves;

even ran up to Felix's bedroom. Where the hell could it be? He looked at his watch and a sick despair seized him. He had only seven minutes left before he must leave the house, and a lot had still to be done.

Good heavens, perhaps it was in Felix's pocket. What a fool not to think of it! Actually he *had* thought of it, but had thrust the idea aside; he didn't want to touch the body. Well, there was no help for it.

In the breast pocket was nothing but a pocket-book. Well, the notes would be useful, anyway. He took them, and thrust the pocket-book roughly back again. Then in the right hand side-pocket of the dinner-jacket his fingers detected an envelope. He pulled it out, and involuntarily gave a whistle of surprise. The envelope had been addressed to himself, and the flap stuck down. He ripped it open. The cheque was inside, enclosed, apparently, in a letter. He heaved a sigh of relief, and thrust the envelope into his own pocket. He had meant to destroy the cheque then and there, but his programme must be slightly modified. The change involved only a very small risk.

He put the spare key back in the top drawer of the writing-table, from which he had originally purloined it; pushed it well to the back amongst some papers in case its loss had been discovered, and in order to suggest that it had been hidden in the drawer all the time. You could not be too careful of details. Then he went to the front door and wedged it carefully open with the door-mat. He went outside and with a stick from the hall smashed a pane of glass in the dining-room window. He thrust in his hand, unlatched the window, and opened it at the bottom. He returned to the house and again shut the front door. This time he brought his shoes in with him.

Hastily he pulled open the sideboard cupboard in the dining-room, seized some spoons and forks, rolled them roughly in a strip of green baize which was in the cupboard, and tossed the package on the table. That was good enough, he thought.

Then back into the study for the last and most unpleasant job.

He lifted his cousin's arm with a reluctant shudder, and turned back the hand of his wrist-watch until it pointed to about five minutes after the time when he, John, had left the pub in the village. He heaved his cousin's body out of the arm-chair and arranged it as well as he could to suggest that he had been standing by the fire-place when he was struck. He laid the body on its right side; the left arm he stretched roughly across the fender, and made sure that the blow had stopped the watch. He stood up again and surveyed the room. He knocked over a small chair, but decided that otherwise his own search had produced an excellent representation of a struggle. The club he left lying by the fire-place.

He looked at his watch. All was well. He was within his scheduled time again. He put on his shoes, tying the bows neatly, despite the involuntary trembling of his hands, and made his exit from the silent house by way of the open window in the dining-room. His jump carried him clear of the narrow flower-bed below the window, on to the flagged path leading from the gate to the front door. Then he ran round the house, back to the garden gate, across the paddock to the left, and so through a well-worn gap in the hedge, into the lane from the village. At this point it dipped between two hills. He took off and pocketed his gloves and then walked quickly on for about thirty yards up the hill in the direction of the village, keeping to the grass by the roadside. He stopped and drew from his pocket a pipe, tobacco-pouch, and a silver match-box. He filled his pipe and struck one of the wax vestas. The wind blew it out at once and he threw it aside. He used three others before his pipe was fairly alight, and then he began to walk slowly back, down the hill towards the house. He walked at the side of the road, and made a point of kicking his shoes on the loose stones. He ought to arrive with dusty shoes, and he was by no means anxious for his second approach to be as silent as his first.

He reached the gate and paused in some anxiety. The relieving constable was due to pass at any moment now. The direction of the wind for the first time became a slight disadvantage. However, he must take no risks. He walked to the front door, rang the bell, waited, and rang again. Then he knocked. After a further interval he walked back towards the gate and listened intently. To his joy, he caught the sound of footsteps. He ran back to the house and shouted, 'Felix! Felix!' in tones of increasing excitement. He heard the footsteps reach the gate and pause. 'Felix! Felix!' he shouted. 'Are you there?'

The gravel scrunched under a pair of heavy boots.

'Anything the matter?' asked a deep, comfortable voice.

'What? Who's that?' John Mansbridge hoped that he had sounded startled.

'Police, sir. What's the trouble?'

John Mansbridge hastily explained his identity.

'This is my cousin's house. Mr Felix Mansbridge.'

'That's right, sir.'

'He asked me to come and see him and stay the night – I do from time to time. Keep a pair of pyjamas here, don't you know, I've just walked up from the station and, well – I can't make him hear – or anyone else. I know he's expecting me. And – look at that!' The constable had reached the door and, urged by the excited cousin, peered at the open window.

'Half a minute,' he said. 'I'll just have a look—'

'Here, I've got a torch,' said John and produced his from his pocket. The constable took it with a word of thanks. He flashed it on the window and gave a grunt of surprise. He seemed uncertain what to do next.

Mansbridge thumped on the knocker again; then the two men strained their ears – or one of them did.

'I wonder if one of the other windows . . .' suggested Mansbridge. The constable leapt at the idea and led the way rapidly round the house until he reached the window through which his companion had peered – oh, years ago, it seemed.

'Looks bad, sir,' said the constable. 'We'd best get round to the front again.' Indeed, the study window was too narrow to admit of entrance.

The constable became a man of action. He bade Mansbridge wait by the door while he climbed in by the window and Mansbridge again reflected with satisfaction that if he had left any traces by either window, the burly constable would have eliminated them pretty completely.

A moment later the door was opened.

'Come in, sir,' the constable whispered hoarsely, 'and wait outside the room where the light is, if you don't mind. I just want to have a look first.'

He walked to the study and half-closed the door behind him. John Mansbridge waited for what seemed an eternity, but in fact was only a few seconds. The constable sized up the situation and returned, switching on the light in the hall. The other man had been fighting to retain control of his nerves, but he was conscious that sweat was pouring down his face. The constable glanced at him with respectful sympathy and muttering, 'Afraid this will be a shock to you, sir,' led the way to the study.

John Mansbridge followed; his return to the horrible scene which he had left only a few minutes before seemed somehow to act as a stimulant to his nerves. His performance of horror and shock was a convincing one, and all the time his inner consciousness was gleefully congratulating him upon it.

'How – how did it happen?' he gasped.

'Ah, queer business,' the constable answered. 'Can't make out what's happened to the room.'

'Yes, but Felix – my cousin?'

'Well, that will have to be seen to,' was the ponderous reply. 'Maybe he smashed himself on the fender there. But it's queer. You see, sir' – he hesitated and then went on – 'it's a case of suicide, seemingly. I found this on the table there, with the glass on it.'

And he held out a sheet of paper, covered with Felix's writing. John stared at it; how in the devil's name had he overlooked the little table? Of course he found the forged cheque before he got as far, but . . .

Through the daze which beset him read the opening words:

'I, Felix Edward Mansbridge, being of sound mind, solemnly declare that I am dying by my own act. I have taken poison. . .'

The room and the paper whirled before his eyes. From a distance he heard the constable say, 'I'll just ring up the station.' Then a 'Hallo,' but addressed, it seemed, not to the Exchange but to himself, and a strong arm lowered him into the very chair where Felix had sat, his bald head just visible. . . .

There was a clink of glass.

'Drink this sir,' said the constable, holding a tumbler to his lips.

'Now let's see where we are,' the superintendent addressed the sergeant and the constable; the latter was manifestly uneasy at the prominence into which his part in the affair had thrust him.

'First, let's fix the known facts about this man, John Mansbridge's, movements. We know the train he came by and the time he left the station; we know he was in the *Four Feathers* just before closing time, and we know he left it and walked past Robson, who was still on duty, in the direction of his cousin's house. There is no turning off the lane, and it's pretty deserted at night. In fact, I doubt if any one uses it except you, Longden. And about forty minutes or three-quarters of an hour after John Mansbridge left the village, you see two or three matches struck as you come down the hill towards the house. And when you get to the house, you find the man hammering at the door. That correct?'

The sergeant and the constable agreed.

'Right. And I may add that we're pretty sure it *was* Mr John Mansbridge who lit his pipe, because he carried a box of wax vestas – not so common these days in country villages – and we found no less than four used matches of the same kind just about the spot where Longden here indicated.'

The constable perked up a little, as if detecting a word of praise for himself.

'All very well and good,' the superintendent continued. 'It certainly looks as if the man walked from the station as said he was going to. Took just the normal time, and his shoes bear out his story. And I don't see how else he could have got there. We may, of course, find someone who met him in the lane, but I should think that unlikely. So much for that.'

He paused for a moment; as if to arrange his thoughts in order, and then resumed his lecture (as it seemed to be).

'Now let's consider this Felix Mansbridge. It seems a pretty clear case of suicide to me – the sergeant made as if to interrupt – but I admit that isn't what we're supposed to think. What we are supposed to think is this; that someone or other broke into the house, began to steal the silver, was disturbed, caught up that club from the hall, knocked the dead man on the head, after a struggle, and decamped. And the broken watch is to suggest that this happened about five minutes after Mr John Mansbridge left the *Four Feathers* and when, consequently, he couldn't be at his cousin's house. I'm afraid I can't swallow that story.'

'You're sure he was poisoned, then, sir?' asked the sergeant.

'Perfectly. And that's not all. In the first place, though, it's not impossible that he was killed in a struggle, it's surprising – considering that the blow was delivered from behind and from above. Then, secondly, there's his confession of suicide. You see, it pretty well fixes the time.'

'How's that, sir?'

'Why, he talked about taking his departure from the world to Wagner's accompaniment.'

'Crazy,' said the sergeant.

'Not in the way you mean. I've no doubt he was thinking of the wireless. You look up last night's programmes and you'll find a Wagner item, and you'll see why, in my opinion, he only took the poison ten minutes after the time shown by the broken watch. And, finally, there's the wound on the head. You take my word, the doctors will find that it was delivered after the man was dead.'

'But why in the name of—'

'Sheer accident, sergeant, in my opinion. Result of sticking to a prearranged plan too closely. Whoever used the club believed that Felix Mansbridge was alive – and that means premeditated murder. Why, in the name of whatever you were going to say, should a burglar suddenly stop his burgling to go into the next room and bash in the head of the owner of the house, and then take to his heels, leaving the swag behind? It stands to reason there never was a burglar at all.'

'Then who'd you reckon it was, sir?'

The superintendent shrugged his shoulders.

'Strictly speaking, I suppose we ought to lay hands on a suspicious fugitive, an unknown visitor,' he said, 'but I fancy it would be sheer waste of time. There was only one visitor – the cousin, John Mansbridge.'

'But his alibi, sir.'

'I know. And I don't see how we're going to break it. All I can say is that *somehow* he got there long before he met you, Longden. And as we can *prove* that he got there some minutes at least before Longden found him at the door, I don't think his alibi holds water after all. I admit I don't see how he rigged it, but I'm satisfied that it's a fake.'

'You can *prove* it, sir?' the sergeant interposed, in a tone which suggested respectful doubt.

'Certainly. For here's a letter which was found in his pocket. It's addressed to him and dated yesterday. The woman who looked after Mr Felix Mansbridge said he wrote a letter before she left, but as he hadn't got a stamp he said it could wait till next day. I haven't a doubt this is the letter – no letter was found in the house ready for post, and you can see that this envelope was addressed *and* gummed down. And the woman says he put the letter in the side pocket of his dinner-jacket – the right side. You'll observe here that if it really was in the right side-pocket it would have been a job to take it out as the body lay, on its right side, in front of the fire-place – in other words, it was taken out before the body lay there. That's a small point, perhaps.'

'The main thing is the letter itself – addressed to John Mansbridge Esq., and found in John Mansbridge Esquire's pocket. I suggest that he found it after the writer was dead, and probably before his body lay on the hearth-rug. For we know that he didn't take the letter while he was in the house with Longden – and therefore he must have done so a good five minutes sooner, and pretty certainly more than that.'

'What's in the letter, sir?' the sergeant inquired.

'A hint of a motive, to put it mildly. It's long; here's the gist of it. Felix says that he has had no answer to his note, and supposes that the cousin can't face him; in other words, he cannot deny the forging of the cheque. Felix says it is hopeless. His cousin will never be convinced that he, Felix, is indeed and in truth a poor man – the large sums mentioned in his father's will were swallowed up by the unpaid debts. Nor, apparently, does the cousin believe that Felix is indeed a sick man. So sick, that though he isn't likely to die next month, the doctors say that he can't live more than a year at the outside. The forgery is the last straw; he's to have no peace in this world, so he'll go to the next, and leave his cousin to inherit his life insurance and what little else there is. And he is not to worry; he will make it quite clear to the police that it was a case of suicide – which, thanks to a special clause, will not invalidate the insurance policy. Oh, yes, he encloses the forged cheque in question, which, he says, he has told the bank is in order. Points to a motive, eh? And makes John Mansbridge's character pretty clear. Thorough wrong 'un.'

There was another pause.

'I see, sir,' the sergeant said slowly. 'And you don't think that John Mansbridge got in quite innocently and found that letter – say, five minutes before Longden saw him light his pipe.'

The superintendent shook his head.

'No, that meeting with Longden, like those calls at the *Four Feathers* and the station, were all part of the man's plan. The pipe-lighting was deliberate – he must have been at pains to observe the exact hour at which Longden walked down that lane. He never thought that out on the spur of the moment.'

Police-constable Longden cleared his throat.

'If I may be so bold, sir, do you mean to say Mr Felix was dead before this Mr John came, and that Mr John smashed his head in, not knowing he was dead already?'

'That's it, in a nutshell, constable. How he got to the house in time, and how he got in, I don't know. Perhaps he had a duplicate key, and chucked it away in the grass somewhere. But in my opinion, however he did it he came down to murder his cousin, and to the best of his belief till you stuck that confession in his hands he *had* murdered his cousin.'

'Thank you, sir. Then to all intents and purposes he was a murderer?'

'I haven't a doubt of it.'

'Well, sir,' and the constable wiped his brow, 'that kind of makes things easier. I don't rightly know what you'll do about it, officially like, but I feel easier in my own mind. I can tell you, sir, when I finished with telephoning and found this Mr John Mansbridge dead in the arm-chair – well, I didn't know whether I was alive or dead meself. Fancy me trying to help him over the shock of seeing his cousin's corpse by giving him a stiff dose of the very same whisky as his cousin had put the poison in. Act of God like, wasn't it, sir?'

He spoke hopefully, with no intention of irreverence.

The Man with the Twisted Lip

Sir Arthur Conan Doyle

Isa Whitney, brother of the late Elias Whitney, D.D., Principal of the Theological College of St George's, was much addicted to opium. The habit grew upon him, as I understand, from some foolish freak when he was at college, for having read De Quincey's description of his dreams and sensations, he had drenched his tobacco with laudanum in an attempt to produce the same effects. He found, as so many more have done, that the practice is easier to attain than to get rid of, and for many years he continued to be a slave to the drug, an object of mingled horror and pity to his friends and relatives. I can see him now, with yellow, pasty face, drooping lids and pin-point pupils, all huddled in a chair, the wreck and ruin of a noble man.

One night – it was in June, '89 – there came a ring to my bell, about the hour when a man gives his first yawn, and glances at the clock. I sat up in my chair, and my wife laid her needlework down in her lap and made a little face of disappointment.

'A patient!' she said. 'You'll have to go out.'

I groaned, for I was newly come back from a weary day.

We heard the door open, a few hurried words, and then quick steps upon the linoleum. Our own door flew open, and a lady, clad in some dark-coloured stuff with a black veil, entered the room.

'You will excuse my calling so late,' she began, and then, suddenly losing her self-control, she ran forward, threw her arms about my wife's neck, and sobbed upon her shoulder. 'Oh! I'm in such trouble!' she cried; 'I do so want a little help.'

'Why,' said my wife, pulling up her veil, 'It is Kate Whitney. How you startled me, Kate! I had not an idea who you were when you came in.'

'I didn't know what to do, so I came straight to you.' That was always the way. Folk who were in grief came to my wife like birds to a lighthouse.

'It was very sweet of you to come. Now, you must have some

wine and water, and sit here comfortably and tell us all about it. Or should you rather that I sent James off to bed?'

'Oh, no, no. I want the Doctor's advice and help too. It's about Isa. He has not been home for two days. I am so frightened about him!'

It was not the first time that she had spoken to us of her husband's trouble, to me as a doctor, to my wife as an old friend and school companion. We soothed and comforted her by such words as we could find. Did she know where her husband was? Was it possible that we could bring him back to her?

It seemed that it was. She had the surest information that of late he had, when the fit was on him, made use of an opium den in the farthest east of the City. Hitherto his orgies had always been confined to one day, and he had come back, twitching and shattered, in the evening. But now the spell had been upon him eight-and-forty hours, and he lay there, doubtless, among the dregs of the docks, breathing in the poison or sleeping off the effects. There he was to be found, she was sure of it, at the 'Bar of Gold', in Upper Swandam Lane. But what was she to do? How could she, a young and timid woman, make her way into such a place, and pluck her husband out from among the ruffians who surrounded him?

There was the case, and of course there was but one way out of it. Might I not escort her to this place? And then, as a second thought, why should she come at all? I was Isa Whitney's medical adviser, and as such I had influence over him. I could manage it better if I were alone. I promised her on my word that I would send him home in a cab within two hours if he were indeed at the address which she had given me. And so in ten minutes I had left my armchair and cheery sitting-room behind me, and was speeding eastward in a hansom on a strange errand, as it seemed to me at the time, though the future only could show how strange it was to be.

But there was no great difficulty in the first stage of my adventure. Upper Swandam Lane is a vile alley lurking behind the high wharves which line the north side of the river to the east of London Bridge. Between a slop shop and a gin shop, approached by a steep flight of steps leading down to a black gap like the mouth of a cave, I found the den of which I was in search. Ordering my cab to wait, I pressed down the steps, worn hollow in the centre by the ceaseless tread of drunken feet, and by the light of a flickering oil lamp above the door I found the latch and made my way into a long, low room, thick and heavy with the brown opium smoke, and terraced with wooden berths, like the forecastle of an emigrant ship.

Through the gloom one could dimly catch a glimpse of bodies lying in strange fantastic poses, bowed shoulders, bent knees, heads thrown back and chins pointing upwards, with here and there a dark, lack-lustre eye turned upon the newcomer. Out of the black shadows there glimmered little red circles of light, now bright, now faint, as the burning poison waxed or waned in the bowls of the metal pipes. The most lay silent, but some muttered to themselves, and others talked together in a strange, low monotonous voice, their conversation coming in gushes, and then suddenly tailing off into silence, each mumbling out his own thoughts, and paying little heed to the words of his neighbour. At the farther end was a small brazier of burning charcoal, beside which on a three-legged stool there sat a tall, thin old man, with his jaw resting upon his two fists, and his elbows upon his knees, staring into the fire.

As I entered, a sallow Malay attendant had hurried up with a pipe for me and a supply of the drug, beckoning me to an empty berth.

'Thank you, I have not come to stay,' said I. 'There is a friend of mine here, Mr Isa Whitney, and I wish to speak with him.'

There was a movement and an exclamation from my right, and peering through the gloom, I saw Whitney, pale, haggard, and unkempt, staring out at me.

'My God! It's Watson,' said he. He was in a pitiable state of reaction, with every nerve in a twitter. 'I say, Watson, what o'clock is it?'

'Nearly eleven.'

'Of what day?'

'Of Friday, June 19th.'

'Good heavens! I thought it was Wednesday. It is Wednesday. What d'you want to frighten a chap for? He sank his face on to his arms, and began to sob in a high treble key.

'I tell you that it is Friday, man. Your wife has been waiting this two days for you. You should be ashamed of yourself!'

'So I am. But you've got mixed, Watson, for I have only been here a few hours, three pipes, four pipes – I forget how many. But I'll go home with you. I wouldn't frighten Kate – poor little Kate. Give me your hand! Have you a cab?'

'Yes, I have one waiting.'

'Then I shall go in it. But I must owe something. Find what I owe, Watson. I am all off colour. I can do nothing for myself.'

I walked down the narrow passage between the double row of sleepers, holding my breath to keep out the vile, stupefying fumes of the drug, and looking about for the manager. As I passed the tall man who sat by the brazier I felt a sudden pluck at my skirt, and a low voice whispered, 'Walk past me, and then look back at me.' The words fell quite distinctly upon my ear. I glanced down. They could only have come from the old man at my side, and yet he sat now as absorbed as ever, very thin, very wrinkled, bent with age, an opium pipe dangling down from between his knees, as though it had dropped in sheer lassitude from his fingers. I took two steps forward and looked back. It took all my self-control to prevent me from breaking out into a cry of astonishment. He had turned his back so that none could see him but I. His form had filled out, his wrinkles were gone, the dull eyes had regained their fire, and there, sitting by the fire, and grinning at my surprise, was none other than Sherlock Holmes. He made a slight motion to me to approach him, and instantly, as he turned his face half-round to the company once more, subsided into a doddering, loose-lipped senility.

'Holmes!' I whispered, 'what on earth are you doing in this den?'

'As low as you can,' he answered, 'I have excellent ears. If you would have the great kindness to get rid of that sottish friend of yours, I should be exceedingly glad to have a little talk with you.'

'I have a cab outside.'

'Then pray send him home in it. You may safely trust him, for he appears to be too limp to get into any mischief. I should recommend you also to send a note by the cabman to your wife to say that you have thrown in your lot with me. If you will wait outside, I shall be with you in five minutes.'

It was difficult to refuse any of Sherlock Holmes's requests, for they were always so exceedingly definite, and put forward with such an air of mastery. I felt, however, that when Whitney was once confined in the cab, my mission was practically accomplished; and for the rest, I could not wish anything better than to be associated with my friend in one of those singular adventures which were the normal condition of his existence. In a few minutes I had written my note, paid Whitney's bill, led him out to the cab, and seen him driven through the darkness. In a very short time a decrepit figure had emerged from the opium den, and I was walking down the street with Sherlock Holmes. For two streets he shuffled along with a bent back and an uncertain foot. Then, glancing quickly round, he straightened himself out and burst into a hearty fit of laughter.

'I suppose, Watson,' said he, 'that you imagine that I have added opium-smoking to cocaine injections and all the other little weaknesses on which you have favoured me with your medical views.'

'I was certainly surprised to find you there.'

'But not more so than I to find you.'

'I came to find a friend.'

'And I to find an enemy!'

'An enemy?'

'Yes, one of my natural enemies, or, shall I say, my natural prey. Briefly, Watson, I am in the midst of a very remarkable inquiry, and I have hoped to find a clue in the incoherent ramblings of these sots, as I have done before now. Had I been recognized in that den my life would not have been worth an hour's purchase, for I have used it before now for my own purposes, and the rascally Lascar who runs it has sworn vengeance upon me. There is a trap-door at the back of that building, near the corner of Paul's Wharf, which could tell some strange tales of what has passed through it upon the moonless nights.'

'What! You do not mean bodies?'

'Aye, bodies, Watson. We should be rich men if we had a thousand pounds for every poor devil who has been done to death in that den. It is the vilest murder-trap on the whole riverside, and I fear Neville St Clair has entered it never to leave it more. But our trap should be here!' He put his two forefingers between his teeth and whistled shrilly, a signal which was answered by a similar whistle from the distance, followed shortly by the rattle of wheels and the clink of horse's hoofs. 'Now, Watson,' said Holmes, as a tall dog-cart dashed up through the gloom, throwing out two golden tunnels of yellow light from its side-lanterns, 'you'll come with me, won't you?'

'If I can be of use.'

'Oh, a trusty comrade is always of use. And a chronicler still more so. My room at the Cedars is a double-bedded one.'

'The Cedars?'

'Yes; that is Mr St Clair's house. I am staying there while I conduct the inquiry.'

'Where it is, then?'

'Near Lee, in Kent. We have a seven-mile drive before us.'

'But I am all in the dark.'

'Of course you are. You'll know all about it presently. Jump up here! All right, John, we shall not need you. Here's half-a-crown. Look out for me tomorrow about eleven. Give her her head! So long, then!'

He flicked the horse with his whip, and we dashed away through the endless succession of sombre and deserted streets, which widened gradually, until we were flying across a broad balustraded bridge, with the murky river flowing sluggishly beneath us. Beyond lay another broad wilderness of bricks and mortar, its silence broken only by the heavy, regular footfall of the policeman, or the songs and shouts of some belated party of revellers. A dull wrack was drifting slowly across the sky, and a star or two twinkled dimly here and there through the rifts of the clouds. Holmes drove in silence, with his head sunk upon his breast, and the air of a man who is lost in thought, whilst I sat beside him curious to learn what this new quest might be which seemed to tax his powers so sorely, and yet afraid to break in upon the current of his thoughts. We had driven several miles, and were beginning to get to the fringe of the belt of suburban villas, when he shook himself, shrugged his shoulders, and lit up his pipe with the air of a man who has satisfied himself that he is acting for the best.

'You have a grand gift of silence, Watson,' said he. 'It makes you quite invaluable as a companion. 'Pon my word, it is a great thing for me to have someone to talk to, for my own thoughts are not over-pleasant. I was wondering what I should say to this dear little woman tonight when she meets me at the door.'

'You forget that I know nothing about it.'

'I shall just have time to tell you the facts of the case before we get to Lee. It seems absurdly simple, and yet, somehow, I can get nothing to go upon. There's plenty of thread, no doubt, but I can't get the end of it in my hand. Now, I'll state the case clearly and concisely to you, Watson, and maybe you may see a spark where all is dark to me.'

'Proceed, then.'

'Some years ago – to be definite, in May 1884 – there came to Lee a gentleman, Neville St Clair by name, who appeared to have plenty of money. He took a large villa, laid out the grounds very nicely, and lived generally in good style. By degrees he made friends in the neighbourhood, and in 1887 he married the daughter of a local brewer, by whom he has now had two children. He had no occupation, but was interested in several companies, and went into town as a rule in the morning, returning by the 5.14 from Cannon Street every night. Mr St Clair is now 37 years of age, is a man of temperate habits, a good husband, a very affectionate father, and a man who is popular with all who know him. I may add that his whole debts at the present moment, as far as we have been able to ascertain amount to £88 10s., while he has £220 standing to his credit in the Capital and Counties Bank. There is no reason, therefore, to think that money troubles have been weighing upon his mind.'

'Last Monday Mr Neville St Clair went into town rather earlier than usual, remarking before he started that he had two important commissions to perform, and that he would bring his little boy home a box of bricks. Now, by the merest chance his wife received a telegram upon this same Monday, very shortly after his departure, to the effect that a small parcel of considerable value which she had been expecting was waiting for her at the offices of the Aberdeen Shipping Company. Now, if you are well up in your London, you will know that the office of the company is in Fresno Street, which branches out of Upper Swandam Lane, where you found me tonight. Mrs St Clair had her lunch, started for the City, did some shopping, proceeded to the Company's office, got her packet, and found herself exactly at 4.35 walking through Swandam Lane on her way back to the station. You have followed me so far?'

'It is very clear.'

'If you remember, Monday was an exceeding hot day, and Mrs St Clair walked slowly, glancing about in the hope of seeing a cab, as she did not like the neighbourhood in which she found herself. While she walked in this way down Swandam Lane she suddenly heard an ejaculation or cry, and was struck cold to see her husband looking down at her, and, as it seemed to her, beckoning to her from a second-floor window. The window was open, and she distinctly saw his face, which she describes as being terribly agitated. He waved his hands frantically to her, and then vanished from the window so suddenly that it seemed to her that he had been plucked back by some irresistible force from behind. One singular point which struck her quick feminine eye was that, although he wore some dark coat, such as he had started to town in, he had on neither collar nor necktie.

'Convinced that something was amiss with him, she rushed down the steps – for the house was none other than the opium den in which you found me tonight – and, running through the front room, she attempted to ascend the stairs which led to the first floor. At the foot of the stairs, however, she met this Lascar scoundrel, of whom I have spoken, who thrust her back, and, aided by a Dane, who acts as assistant there, pushed her out into the street. Filled with the most maddening doubts and fears, she rushed down the lane, and, by rare good fortune, met, in Fresno Street, a number of constables with an inspector, all on their way to their beat. The inspector and two men accompanied her back, and, in spite of the continued resistance of the proprietor, they made their way to the room in which Mr St Clair had last been seen. There was no sign of him there. In fact, in the whole of that floor there was no one to be found, save a crippled wretch of hideous aspect, who, it seems, made his home there. Both he and Lascar stoutly swore that no one else had been in the front room during that afternoon. So determined was their denial that the inspector was staggered, and had almost come to believe that Mrs St Clair had been deluded when, with a cry, she sprang at a small deal box which lay upon the table, and tore the lid from it. Out there fell a cascade of children's bricks. It was the toy which he had promised to bring home.'

'This discovery, and the evident confusion which the cripple showed, made the inspector realize that the matter was serious. The rooms were carefully examined, and results all pointed to an abominable crime. The front room was plainly furnished as a sitting-room, and led into a small bedroom, which looked out upon the back of one of the wharves. Between the wharf and the bedroom window is a narrow strip, which is dry at low tide, but is covered at high tide with at least four and a half feet of water. The bedroom window was a broad one, and opened from below. On examination traces of blood were to be seen upon the window-sill, and several scattered drops were visible upon the wooden floor of the bedroom. Thrust away behind a curtain in the front room were all the clothes of Mr Neville St Clair, with the exception of his coat. His boots, his socks, his hat, and his watch – all were there. There were no signs of violence upon any of these garments, and there were no other traces of Mr Neville St Clair. Out of the window he must apparently have gone, for no other exit could be discovered, and the ominous bloodstains upon the sill gave little promise that he could save himself by swimming, for the tide was at its very highest at the moment of the tragedy.

'And now as to the villains who seemed to be immediately implicated in the matter. The Lascar was known to be a man of the vilest antecedents, but as by Mrs St Clair's story he was known to have been at the foot of the stair within a few seconds of her husband's appearance at the window, he could hardly have been more than an accessory to the crime. His defence was one of absolute ignorance, and he protested that he had no knowledge as to the doings of Hugh Boone, his lodger, and that he could not account in any way for the presence of the missing gentleman's clothes.

'So much for the Lascar manager. Now for the sinister cripple who lives upon the second floor of the opium den, and who was certainly the last human being whose eyes rested upon Neville St Clair. His name is Hugh Boone, and his hideous face is one which is familiar to every man who goes much to the City. He is a professional beggar, though in order to avoid the police regulations he pretends to a small trade in wax vestas. Some little distance down Threadneedle Street upon the left-hand side there is, as you may have remarked, a small angle in the wall. Here it is that the creature takes his daily seat, cross-legged, with his tiny stock of matches on his lap, and as he is a piteous spectacle a small rain of charity descends into the greasy leather cap which lies upon the pavement before him. I have watched this fellow more than once, before ever I thought of making his professional acquaintance, and I have been surprised at the harvest which he has reaped in so short a time. His appearance, you see, is so remarkable that no one can pass him without observing him. A shock of orange hair, a pale face disfigured by a horrible scar, which, by its contraction, has turned up the outer edge of his upper lip, a bull-dog chin, and a pair of very penetrating dark eyes, which present a singular contrast to the colour of his hair, all mark him out from amid the common crowd of mendicants, and so, too, does his wit, for he is ever ready with a reply to any piece of chaff which may be thrown at him by the passers-by. This is the man whom we now learn to have been the lodger at the opium den, and to have been the last man to see the gentleman of whom we are in quest.'

'But a cripple!' said I. 'What could he have done single-handed against a man in the prime of life?'

'He is a cripple in the sense that he walks with a limp; but, in other respects, he appears to be a powerful and well-nurtured man. Surely your medical experience would tell you, Watson, that weakness in one limb is often compensated for by exceptional strength in the others.'

'Pray continue your narrative.'

'Mrs St Clair had fainted at the sight of the blood upon the window, and she was escorted home in a cab by the police, as her presence could be of no help to them in their investigations. Inspector Barton, who had charge of the case, made a very careful examination of the premises, but without finding anything which threw any light upon the matter. One mistake had been made in not arresting Boone instantly, as he was allowed some few minutes during which he might have communicated with his friend Lascar, but this fault was soon remedied, and he was seized and searched, without anything being found which could incriminate him. There were, it is true, some bloodstains upon his right shirt-sleeve, but he pointed to his ring finger, which had been cut near the nail, and explained that the bleeding came from there, adding that he had been to the window not long before, and that the stains which had been observed there came doubtless from the same source. He denied strenuously having ever seen Mr Neville St Clair, and swore that the presence of the clothes in his room was as much a mystery to him as to the police. As to Mrs St Clair's assertion, that she had actually seen her husband at the window, he declared that she must have been either mad or dreaming. He was removed, loudly protesting, to the police station, while the inspector remained upon the premises in the hope that the ebbing tide might afford some fresh clue.'

'And it did, though they hardly found upon the mudbank what they had feared to find. It was Neville St Clair's coat, and not Neville St Clair, which lay uncovered as the tide receded. And what do you think they found in the pockets?'

'I cannot imagine.'

'No, I don't think you will guess. Every pocket stuffed with pennies and halfpennies – four hundred and twenty-one pennies, and two hundred and seventy halfpennies. It was no wonder that it had not been swept away by the tide. But a human body is a different matter. There is a fierce eddy between the wharf and the house. It seemed likely enough that the weighted coat had remained when the stripped body had been sucked away into the river.'

'But I understand that all the other clothes were found in the room. Would the body be dressed in a coat alone?'

'No, sir, but the facts might be met speciously enough. Suppose that this man Boone had thrust Neville St Clair through the window, there is no human eye which could have seen the deed. What would he do then? It would of course instantly strike him that he must get rid of the tell-tale garments. He would seize the coat then, and be in the act of throwing it out when it would occur to him that it would swim and not sink. He has little time, for he had heard the scuffle downstairs when the wife tried to force her way up, and perhaps he has already heard from his Lascar confederate that the police are hurrying up the street. There is not an instant to be lost. He rushes to some secret hoard, where he has accumulated the fruits of his beggary, and he stuffs all the coins upon which he can lay his hands into the pockets to make sure of the coat's sinking. He throws it out, and would have done the same with the other garments had not he heard the rush of steps below, and only just had time to close the window when the police appeared.'

'It certainly sounds feasible.'

'Well, we will take it as a working hypothesis for want of a better. Boone, as I have told you, was arrested and taken to the station, but it could not be shown that there had ever been anything against him. He had for years been known as a professional beggar, but his life appeared to have been a very quiet and innocent one. There the matter stands at present, and the questions which have to be solved, what Neville St Clair was doing in the opium den, what happened to him when there, where he is now, and what Hugh Boone had to do with his disappearance, are all as far from solution as ever. I confess that I cannot recall any case within my experience which looked at the first glance so simple, and yet which presented such difficulties.'

Whilst Sherlock Holmes had been detailing this singular series of events we had been whirling through the outskirts of the great town until the last straggling houses had been left behind, and we rattled along with a country hedge upon either side of us. Just as he finished, however, we drove through two scattered villages, where a few lights still glimmered in the windows.

'We are on the outskirts of Lee,' said my companion. 'We have touched on three English counties in our short drive, starting in Middlesex, passing over an angle of Surrey, and ending in Kent. See that light among the trees? That is the Cedars, and beside that lamp sits a woman whose anxious ears have already, I have little doubt, caught the clink of our horse's feet.'

'But why are you not conducting the case from Baker Street?' I asked.

'Because there are many inquiries which must be made out here. Mrs St Clair has most kindly put two rooms at my disposal, and you may rest assured that she will have nothing but a welcome for my friend and colleague. I hate to meet her, Watson, when I have no news of her husband. Here we are. Whoa, there, whoa!'

We had pulled up in front of a large villa which stood within its own grounds. A stable-boy had run out to the horse's head, and, springing down, I followed Holmes up the small, winding gravel drive which led to the house. As we approached, the door flew open, and a little blonde woman stood in the opening, clad in some sort of light *mousseline-de-soie*, with a touch of fluffy pink chiffon at her neck and wrists. She stood with her figure outlined against the flood of light, one hand upon the door, one half raised in eagerness, her body slightly bent, her head and face protruded, with eager eyes and parted lips, a standing question.

'Well?' she cried, 'well?' And then, seeing that there were two of us, she gave a cry of hope which sank into a groan as she saw that my companion shook his head and shrugged his shoulders.

'No good news?'

'None.'

'No bad?'

'No.'

'Thank God for that. But come in. You must be weary, for you have had a long day.'

'This is my friend, Dr Watson. He has been of most vital use to me in several of my cases, and a lucky chance has made it possible for me to bring him out and associate him with this investigation.'

'I am delighted to see you,' said she, pressing my hand warmly. 'You will, I am sure, forgive anything which may be wanting in our arrangements, when you consider the blow which has come so suddenly upon us.'

'My dear madam,' said I, 'I am an old campaigner, and if I were not, I can very well see that no apology is needed. If I can be of any assistance, either to you or to my friend here, I shall be indeed happy.'

'Now, Mr Sherlock Holmes,' said the lady as we entered a well-lit dining-room, upon the table of which a cold supper had been laid out. 'I should very much like to ask you one or two plain questions, to which I beg you will give a plain answer.'

'Certainly, madam.'

'Do not trouble about my feelings. I am not hysterical, nor given to fainting. I simply wish to hear your real, real opinion.'

'Upon what point?'

'In your heart of hearts, do you think that Neville is alive?'

Sherlock Holmes seemed to be embarrassed by the question. 'Frankly now!' she repeated, standing upon the rug, and looking keenly down at him, as he leaned back in a basket chair.

'Frankly, then, madam, I do not.'

'You think that he is dead?'

'I do.'

'Murdered?'

'I don't say that. Perhaps.'

'And on what day did he meet his death?'

'On Monday.'

'Then perhaps, Mr Holmes, you will be good enough to explain how it is that I have received this letter from him today?'

Sherlock Holmes sprang out of his chair as if he had been galvanized.

'What!' he roared.

'Yes, today.' She stood smiling, holding up a little slip of paper in the air.'

'May I see it?'

'Certainly.'

He snatched it from her in his eagerness, and smoothing it out upon the table, he drew over the lamp, and examined it intently. I had left my chair, and was gazing at it over his shoulder. The envelope was a very coarse one, and was stamped with the Gravesend postmark, and with the date of that very day, or rather of the day before, for it was considerably after midnight.

'Coarse writing!' murmured Holmes. 'Surely this is not your husband's writing, madam.'

'No, but the enclosure is.'

'I perceive also that whoever addressed the envelope had to go and inquire as to the address.'

'How can you tell that?'

'The name, you see, is in perfectly black ink, which has dried itself. The rest is of the greyish colour which shows that blotting-paper had been used. If it had been written straight off, and then blotted, none would be of a deep black shade. This man has written the name, and there has then been a pause before he wrote the address, which can only mean that he was not familiar with it. It is, of course, a trifle, but there is nothing so important as trifles. Let us now see the letter! Ha! there has been an enclosure here!'

'Yes, there was a ring. His signet ring.'

'And you are sure that this is your husband's hand?'

'One of his hands.'

'One?'

'His hand when he wrote hurriedly. It is very unlike his usual writing, and yet I know it well.'

' "Dearest, do not be frightened. All will come well. There is a huge error which it may take some little time to rectify. Wait in patience. – Neville." Written in pencil upon a flyleaf of a book, octavo size, no watermark. Posted today in Gravesend by a man with a dirty thumb. Ha! And the flap has been gummed, if I am not very much in error, by a person who has been chewing tobacco. And you have no doubt that it is your husband's hand, madam?'

'None. Neville wrote those words.'

'And they were posted today at Gravesend. Well, Mrs St Clair, the clouds lighten, though I should not venture to say that the danger is over.'

'But he must be alive, Mr Holmes.'

'Unless this is a clever forgery to put us on the wrong scent. The ring, after all, proves nothing. It may have been taken from him.'

'No, no; it is, it is, it is his very own writing!'

'Very well. It may, however, have been written on Monday, and only posted today.'

'That is possible.'

'If so, much may have happened between.'

'Oh, you must not discourage me, Mr Holmes. I know that all is well with him. There is so keen a sympathy between us that I should know if evil came upon him. On the very day that I saw him last he cut himself in the bedroom, and yet I in the dining-room rushed upstairs instantly with the utmost certainty that something had happened. Do you think that I would respond to such a trifle, and yet be ignorant of his death?'

'I have seen too much not to know that the impression of a woman may be more valuable than the conclusion of an analytical reasoner. And in this letter you certainly have a very strong piece of evidence to corroborate your view. But if your husband is alive and able to write letters, why should he remain away from you?'

'I cannot imagine. It is unthinkable.'

'And on Monday he made no remarks before leaving you?'

'No.'

'And you were surprised to see him in Swandam Lane?'

'Very much so.'

'Was the window open?'

'Yes.'

'Then he might have called to you?'

'He might.'

'He only, as I understand, gave an inarticulate cry?'

'Yes.'

'A call for help, you thought?'

'Yes. He waved his hands.'

'But it might have been a cry of surprise. Astonishment at the unexpected sight of you might cause him to throw up his hands.'

'It is possible.'

'And you thought he was pulled back?'

'He disappeared so suddenly.'

'He might have leaped back. You did not see anyone else in the room?'

'No, but this horrible man confessed to having been there, and the Lascar was at the foot of the stairs.'

'Quite so. Your husband, as far as you could see, had his ordinary clothes on?'

'But without his collar or tie. I distinctly saw his bare throat.'

'Had he ever spoken of Swandam Lane?'

'Never.'

'Had he ever shown signs of having taken opium?'

'Never.'

'Thank you, Mrs St Clair. Those are the principal points about which I wished to be absolutely clear. We shall now have a little supper and then retire, for we may have a very busy day tomorrow.'

A large and comfortable double-bedded room had been placed at our disposal, and I was quickly between the sheets, for I was weary after my night of adventure. Sherlock Holmes was a man, however, who when he had an unsolved problem upon his mind would go for days, and even for a week, without rest, turning it over, rearranging his facts, looking at it from every point of view, until he had either fathomed it, or convinced himself that his data were insufficient. It was soon evident to me that he was now preparing for an all-night sitting. He took off his coat and waistcoat, put on a large blue dressing-gown, and then wandered about the room collecting pillows from his bed, and cushions from the sofa and armchairs. With these he constructed a sort of Eastern divan, upon which he perched himself crosslegged, with an ounce of shag tobacco and a box of matches laid out in front of him. In the dim light of the lamp I saw him sitting there, an old brier pipe between his lips, his eyes fixed vacantly upon the corner of the ceiling, the blue smoke curling up from him, silent, motionless, with the light shining upon his strong-set aquiline features. So he sat as I dropped off to sleep, and so he sat when a sudden ejaculation caused me to wake up, and I found the summer sun shining into the apartment. The pipe was still between his lips, the smoke still curled upwards, and the room was full of a dense tobacco haze, but nothing remained of the heap of shag which I had seen upon the previous night.

'Awake, Watson?' he asked.

'Yes.'

'Game for a morning drive?'

'Certainly.'

'Then dress. No one is stirring yet, but I know where the stable-boy sleeps, and we shall soon have the trap out.' He chuckled to himself as he spoke, his eyes twinkled, and he seemed a different man to the sombre thinker of the previous night.

As I dressed I glanced at my watch. It was no wonder that no one was stirring. It was twenty-five minutes past four. I had hardly finished when Holmes returned with the news that the boy was putting in the horse.

'I want to test a little theory of mine,' said he, pulling on his boots. 'I think, Watson, that you are now standing in the presence of one of the most absolute fools in Europe. I deserve to be kicked from here to Charing Cross. But I think I have the key of the affair now.'

'And where is it?' I asked, smiling.

'In the bathroom,' he answered. 'Oh, yes, I am not joking,' he continued, seeing my look of incredulity. 'I have just been there, and I have taken it out, and I have got it in this Gladstone bag. Come on, my boy, and we shall see whether it will not fit the lock.'

We made our way downstairs as quietly as possible; and out into the bright morning sunshine. In the road stood our horse and trap, with the half-clad stable-boy waiting at the head. We both sprang in, and away we dashed down the London road. A few country carts were stirring, bearing in vegetables to the metropolis, but the lines of villas on either side were as silent and lifeless as some city in a dream.

'It has been in some points a singular case,' said Holmes, flicking the horse on into a gallop. 'I confess that I have been as blind as a mole, but it is better to learn wisdom late, than never to learn it at all.'

In town, the earliest risers were just beginning to look sleepily from their windows as we drove through the streets of the Surrey side. Passing down the Waterloo Bridge Road we crossed over the river, and dashing up Wellington Street wheeled sharply to the right, and found ourselves in Bow Street. Sherlock Holmes was well known to the force, and the two constables at the door saluted him. One of them held the horse's head while the other led us in.

'Who is on duty?' asked Holmes.

'Inspector Bradstreet, sir.'

'Ah, Bradstreet, how are you?' A tall, stout official had come down the stone-flagged passage, in a peaked cap and frogged jacket. 'I wish to have a word with you, Bradstreet.'

'Certainly, Mr Holmes. Step into my room here.'

It was a small office-like room, with a huge ledger upon the table, and a telephone projecting from the wall. The inspector sat down at his desk.

'What can I do for you, Mr Holmes?'

'I called about that beggar-man, Boone – the one who was charged with being concerned in the disappearance of Mr Neville St Clair, of Lee.'

'Yes. He was brought up and remanded for further inquiries.'

'So I heard. You have him here?'

'In the cells.'

'Is he quiet?'

'Oh, he gives no trouble. But he is a dirty scoundrel.'

'Dirty?'

'Yes, it is all we can do to make him wash his hands, and his face is as black as a tinker's. Well, when once his case has been settled he will have a regular prison bath; and I think, if you saw him you would agree with me that he needed it.'

'I should like to see him very much.'

'Would you? That is easily done. Come this way. You can leave your bag.'

'No, I think I'll take it.'

'Very good. Come this way, if you please.' He led us down a passage, opened a barred door, passed down a winding stair, and brought us to a whitewashed corridor with a line of doors on each side.

'The third on the right is his,' said the inspector. 'Here it is!' He quietly shot back a panel in the upper part of the door, and glanced through.

'He is asleep,' said he. 'You can see him very well.'

We both put our eyes to the grating. The prisoner lay with his face towards us, in a very deep sleep, breathing slowly and heavily. He was a middle-sized man, coarsely clad as became his calling, with a coloured shirt protruding through the rent in his tattered coat. He was, as the inspector had said, extremely dirty, but the grime which covered his face could not conceal its repulsive ugliness. A broad weal from an old scar ran across it from eye to chin, and by its contraction had turned up one side of the upper lip, so that three teeth were exposed in a perpetual snarl. A shock of very bright red hair grew low over his eyes and forehead.

'He's a beauty, isn't he?' said the inspector.

'He certainly needs a wash,' remarked Holmes. 'I had an idea that he might and I took the liberty of bringing the tools with me.' He opened his Gladstone bag as he spoke, and took out, to my astonishment, a very large bath sponge.

'He! he! You are a funny one,' chuckled the inspector.

'Now, if you will have the great goodness to open that door very quietly, we will soon make him cut a much more respectable figure.'

'Well, I don't know why not,' said the inspector. 'He doesn't look a credit to the Bow Street cells, does he?' He slipped his key into the lock, and we all very quietly entered the cell. The sleeper half turned, and then settled down once more into a deep slumber. Holmes stooped to the water jug, moistened his sponge, and then rubbed it twice vigorously across and down the prisoner's face.

'Let me introduce you,' he shouted, 'to Mr Neville St Clair, of Lee, in the county of Kent.'

Never in my life have I seen such a sight. The man's face peeled off under the sponge like the bark from a tree. Gone was the coarse brown tint! Gone, too, the horrid scar which had seamed it across, and the twisted lip which had given the repulsive sneer to the face! A twitch brought away the tangled red hair, and there, sitting up in his bed, was a pale, sad-faced, refined-looking man, black-haired and smooth-skinned, rubbing his eyes, and staring about him with sleepy bewilderment. Then suddenly realizing his exposure, he broke into a scream, and threw himself down with his face to the pillow.

'Great heaven!' cried the inspector, 'it is, indeed, the missing man. I know him from the photograph.'

The prisoner turned with the reckless air of man who abandons himself to his destiny. 'Be it so,' said he. 'And pray what am I charged with?'

'With making away with Mr Neville St – Oh, come, you can't be charged with that, unless they make a case of attempted suicide of it,' said the inspector, with a grin. 'Well, I have been twenty-seven years in the Force, but this really takes the cake.'

'If I am Mr Neville St Clair, then it is obvious that no crime has been committed, and that, therefore, I am illegally detained.'

'No crime, but a very great error has been committed,' said Holmes. 'You would have done better to have trusted your wife.'

'It was not the wife, it was the children,' groaned the prisoner.

'God help me, I would not have them ashamed of their father. My God! What an exposure! What can I do?'

Sherlock Holmes sat down beside him on the couch, and patted him kindly on the shoulder.

'If you leave it to a court of law to clear the matter up,' said he, 'of course you can hardly avoid publicity. On the other hand, if you convince the police authorities that there is no possible case against you, I do not know that there is any reason that the details should find their way into the papers. Inspector Bradstreet would, I am sure, make notes upon anything which you might tell us, and submit it to the proper authorities. The case would then never go into court at all.'

'God bless you!' cried the prisoner passionately. 'I would have endured imprisonment, aye, even execution, rather than have left my miserable secret as a family blot to my children.

'You are the first who have ever heard my story. My father was a schoolmaster in Chesterfield, where I received an excellent education. I travelled in my youth, took to the stage, and finally became a reporter on an evening paper in London. One day my editor wished to have a series of articles upon begging in the metropolis, and I volunteered to supply them. There was the point from which all my adventures started. It was only by trying begging as an amateur that I could get the facts upon which to base my articles. When an actor I had, of course, learned all the secrets of making up, and had been famous in the green-room for my skill. I took advantage now of my attainments. I painted my face, and to make myself as pitiable as possible I made a good scar and fixed one side of my lip in a twist by the aid of a small slip of flesh-coloured plaster. Then with a red head of hair, and an appropriate dress, I took my station in the busiest part of the City, ostensibly as a match-seller, but really as a beggar. For seven hours I plied my trade, and when I returned home in the evening I found, to my surprise, that I had received no less than twenty-six shillings and fourpence.

'I wrote my articles, and thought little more of the matter until, some time later, I backed a bill for a friend, and had a writ served upon me for £25. I was at my wit's end where to get the money, but a sudden idea came to me. I begged a fortnight's grace from the creditor, asked for a holiday from my employers, and spent the time in begging in the City under my disguise. In ten days I had the money, and had paid the debt.

'Well, you can imagine how hard it was to settle down to arduous work at two pounds a week, when I knew that I could earn as much in a day by smearing my face with a little paint, laying my cap on the ground, and sitting still. It was a long fight between my pride and the money, but the dollars won at last, and I threw up reporting, and sat day after day in the corner which I had chosen, inspiring pity by my ghastly face and filling my pockets with coppers. Only one man knew my secret. He was the keeper of a low den in which I used to lodge in Swandam Lane, where I could every morning emerge as a squalid beggar and in the evening transform myself into a well-dressed man about town. This fellow, a Lascar, was well paid by me for his rooms, so that I knew that my secret was safe in his possession.

'Well, very soon I found that I was saving considerable sums of money. I do not mean that any beggar in the streets of London could earn seven hundred pounds a year – which is less than my average takings – but I had exceptional advantages in my power of making up, and also in a facility of repartee, which improved by practice, and made me quite a recognized character in the City. All day a stream of pennies, varied by silver, poured in upon me, and it was a very bad day upon which I failed to take two pounds.

'As I grew richer I grew more ambitious, took a house in the country, eventually married, without anyone having a suspicion as to my real occupation. My dear wife knew that I had business in the City. She little knew what.

'Last Monday I had finished for the day, and was dressing in my room above the opium den, when I looked out of the window, and saw, to my horror and astonishment, that my wife was standing in the street, with her eyes fixed full upon me. I gave a cry of surprise, threw up my arms to cover my face, and rushing to my confidant, the Lascar, entreated him to prevent anyone from coming up to me. I heard her voice downstairs, but I knew that she could not ascend. Swiftly I threw off my clothes, pulled on those of a beggar, and put on my pigments and wig. Even a wife's eyes could not pierce so complete a disguise. But then it occurred to me that there might be a search in the room and that the clothes might betray me. I threw open the window, re-opening by my violence a small cut which I had inflicted upon myself in the bedroom that morning. Then I seized my coat, which was weighted by the coppers which I had just transferred to it from the leather bag in which I carried my takings. I hurled it out of the window, and it disappeared into the Thames. The other clothes would have followed, but at that moment there was a rush of constables up the stairs, and a few minutes after I found, rather, I confess, to my relief, that instead of being identified as Mr Neville St Clair, I was arrested as his murderer.

'I do not know that there is anything else for me to explain. I was determined to preserve my disguise as long as possible, and hence my preference for a dirty face. Knowing that my wife would be terrible anxious, I slipped off my ring, and confided it to the Lascar at a moment when no constable was watching me, together with a hurried scrawl, telling her that she had no cause to fear.'

'That note only reached her yesterday,' said Holmes.

'Good God! What a week she must have spent.'

'The police have visited this Lascar,' said Inspector Brad-street, 'and I can quite understand that he might find it difficult to post a letter unobserved. Probably he handed it to some sailor customer of his, who forgot all about it for some days.'

'That was it,' said Holmes, nodding approvingly, 'I have no doubt of it. But have you never been prosecuted for begging?'

'Many times; but what was a fine to me?'

'It must stop here, however,' said Bradstreet. 'If the police are to hush this thing up, there must be no more of Hugh Boone.'

'I have sworn it by the most solemn oaths which a man can take.'

'In that case I think that it is probable that no further steps may be taken. But if you are found again, then all must come out. I am sure, Mr Holmes, that we are very much indebted to you for having cleared the matter up. I wish I knew how you reach your results.'

'I reached this one,' said my friend, 'by sitting upon five pillows and consuming an ounce of shag. I think, Watson, that if we drive to Baker Street we shall just be in time for breakfast.'

The Case for the Defence

Graham Greene

It was the strangest murder trial I ever attended. They named it the Peckham murder in the headlines, though Northwood Street, where the old woman was found battered to death, was not strictly speaking in Peckham. This was not one of those cases of circumstantial evidence, in which you feel the jurymen's anxiety – because mistakes *have* been made – like domes of silence muting the court. No, this murderer was all but found with the body; no one present when the Crown counsel outlined his case believed that the man in the dock stood any chance at all.

He was a heavy stout man with bulging bloodshot eyes. All his muscles seemed to be in his thighs. Yes, an ugly customer, one you wouldn't forget in a hurry – and that was an important point because the Crown proposed to call four witnesses who hadn't forgotten him, who had seen him hurrying away from the little red villa in Northwood Street. The clock had just struck two in the morning.

Mrs Salmon in 15 Northwood Street had been unable to sleep; she heard a door click shut and thought it was her own gate. So she went to the window and saw Adams (that was his name) on the steps of Mrs Parker's house. He had just come out and he was wearing gloves. He had a hammer in his hand and she saw him drop it into the laurel bushes by the front gate. But before he moved away, he had looked up – at her window. The fatal instinct that tells a man when he is watched exposed him in the light of a street-lamp to her gaze – his eyes suffused with horrifying and brutal fear, like an animal's when you raise a whip. I talked afterwards to Mrs Salmon, who naturally after the astonishing verdict went in fear herself. As I imagine did all the witnesses – Henry MacDougall, who had been driving home from Benfleet late and nearly ran Adams down at the corner of

Northwood Street. Adams was walking in the middle of the road looking dazed. And old Mr Wheeler, who lived next door to Mrs Parker, at No. 12, and was wakened by a noise – like a chair falling – through the thin-as-paper villa wall, and got up and looked out of the window, just as Mrs Salmon had done, saw Adams's back and, as he turned, those bulging eyes. In Laurel Avenue he had been seen by yet another witness – his luck was badly out; he might as well have committed the crime in broad daylight.

'I understand,' counsel said, 'that the defence proposes to plead mistaken identity. Adams's wife will tell you that he was with her at two in the morning on February 14, but after you have heard the witnesses for the Crown and examined carefully the features of the prisoner, I do not think you will be prepared to admit the possibility of a mistake.'

It was all over, you would have said, but the hanging.

After the formal evidence had been given by the policeman who had found the body and the surgeon who examined it, Mrs Salmon was called. She was the ideal witness, with her slight Scotch accent and her expression of honesty, care and kindness.

The counsel for the Crown brought the story gently out. She spoke very firmly. There was no malice in her, and no sense of importance at standing there in the Central Criminal Court with a judge in scarlet hanging on her words and the reporters writing them down. Yes, she said, and then she had gone downstairs and rung up the police station.

'And do you see the man here in court?'

She looked straight across at the big man in the dock, who stared hard at her with his pekingese eyes without emotion.

'Yes,' she said, 'there he is.'

'You are quite certain?'

She said simply, 'I couldn't be mistaken, sir.'

It was all as easy as that.

'Thank you, Mrs Salmon.'

Counsel for the defence rose to cross-examine. If you had reported as many murder trials as I have, you would have known beforehand what line he would take. And I was right, up to a point.

'Now, Mrs Salmon, you must remember that a man's life may depend on your evidence.'

'I do remember it, sir.'

'Is your eyesight good?'

'I have never had to wear spectacles, sir.'

'You are a woman of fifty-five?'

'Fifty-six, sir.'

'And the man you saw was on the other side of the road?'

'Yes, sir.'

'And it was two o'clock in the morning. You must have remarkable eyes, Mrs Salmon?'

'No, sir. There was moonlight, and when the man looked up, he had the lamplight on his face.'

'And you have no doubt whatever that the man you saw is the prisoner?'

I couldn't make out what he was at. He couldn't have expected any other answer than the one he got.

'None whatever, sir. It isn't a face one forgets.'

Counsel took a look round the court for a moment. Then he said: 'Do you mind, Mrs Salmon, examining again the people in court? No, not the prisoner. Stand up, please, Mr Adams,' and there at the back of the court, with thick stout body and muscular legs and a pair of bulging eyes, was the exact image of the man in the dock. He was even dressed the same – tight blue suit and striped tie.

'Now think very carefully, Mrs Salmon. Can you still swear that the man you saw drop the hammer in Mrs Parker's garden was the prisoner – and not this man, who is his twin brother?'

Of course she couldn't. She looked from one to the other and didn't say a word.

There the big brute sat in the dock with his legs crossed and there he stood too at the back of the court and they both stared at Mrs Salmon. She shook her head.

What we saw then was the end of the case. There wasn't a

witness prepared to swear that it was the prisoner he'd seen. And the brother? He had his alibi, too; he was with his wife.

And so the man was acquitted for lack of evidence. But whether – if he did the murder and not his brother – he was punished or not, I don't know. That extraordinary day had an extraordinary end. I followed Mrs Salmon out of court and we got wedged in the crowd who were waiting, of course, for the twins. The police tried to drive the crowd away, but all they could do was keep the roadway clear for traffic. I learned later that they tried to get the twins to leave by a back way, but they wouldn't. One of them – no one knew which – said, 'I've been acquitted, haven't I?' and they walked bang out the front entrance. Then it happened. I don't know how; though I was only six feet away. The crowd moved and somehow one of the twins got pushed on to the road right in front of a bus.

He gave a squeal like a rabbit and that was all; he was dead, his skull smashed just as Mrs Parker's had been. Divine vengeance? I wish I knew. There was the other Adams getting on his feet from beside the body and looking straight over at Mrs Salmon. He was crying, but whether he was the murderer or the innocent man, nobody will ever be able to tell. But if you were Mrs Salmon, could you sleep at night?

Philomel Cottage

Agatha Christie

'Good-bye, darling.'

'Good-bye, sweetheart.'

Alix Martin stood leaning over the small rustic gate, watching the retreating figure of her husband as he walked down the road in the direction of the village.

Presently he turned a bend and was lost to sight, but Alix still stayed in the same position, absent-mindly smoothing a lock of the rich brown hair which had blown across her face, her eyes far away and dreamy.

Alix Martin was not beautiful, nor even, strictly speaking, pretty. But her face, the face of a woman no longer in her first youth, was irradiated and softened until her former colleagues of the old office days would hardly have recognized her. Miss Alix King had been a trim business-like young woman, efficient, slightly brusque in manner, obviously capable and matter-of-fact.

Alix had graduated in a hard school. For fifteen years, from the age of eighteen until she was thirty-three, she had kept herself (and for seven years of the time an invalid mother) by her work as a shorthand-typist. It was the struggle for existence which had hardened the soft lines of her girlish face.

True, there had been romance – of a kind – Dick Windyford, a fellow clerk. Very much of a woman at heart, Alix had always known without seeming to know that he cared. Outwardly they had been friends, nothing more. Out of his slender salary Dick had been hard put to it to provide for the schooling of a younger brother. For the moment he could not think of marriage.

And then suddenly deliverance from daily toil had come to the girl in the most unexpected manner. A distant cousin had died, leaving her money to Alix – a few thousand pounds, enough to bring in a couple of hundred a year. To Alix it was freedom, life, independence. Now she and Dick need wait no longer.

But Dick reacted unexpectedly. He had never directly spoken of his love to Alix; now he seemed less inclined to do so than ever. He avoided her, became morose and gloomy. Alix was quick to realize the truth. She had become a woman of means. Delicacy and pride stood in the way of Dick asking her to be his wife.

She liked him none the worse for it, and was indeed deliberating as to whether she herself might not take the first step, when for the second time the unexpected descended upon her.

She met Gerald Martin at a friend's house. He fell violently in love with her, and within a week they were engaged. Alix, who had always considered herself, 'not the falling-in-love kind,' was swept clean off her feet.

Unwittingly she had found the way to arouse her former lover. Dick Windyford had come to her stammering with rage and anger.

'The man's a perfect stranger to you! You know nothing about him!'

'I know that I love him.'

'How can you know – in a week?'

'It doesn't take every one eleven years to find out that they're in love with a girl,' cried Alix angrily.

His face went white.

'I've cared for you ever since I met you. I thought that you cared also.'

Alix was truthful.

'I thought so too,' she admitted. 'But that was because I didn't know what love was.'

Then Dick burst out again. Prayers, entreaties, even threats – threats against the man who had supplanted him. It was amazing to Alix to see the volcano that existed beneath the reserved exterior of the man she had thought she knew so well.

Her thoughts went back to that interview now, on this sunny morning, as she leant on the gate of the cottage. She had been married a month, and she was idyllically happy. Yet, in the momentary absence of her husband who was everything to her, a tinge of anxiety invaded her perfect happiness. And the cause of that anxiety was Dick Windyford.

Three times since her marriage she had dreamed the same dream. The environment differed, but the main facts were always the same. *She saw her husband lying dead and Dick Windyford standing over him, and she knew clearly and distinctly that his was the hand which had dealt the fatal blow.*

But horrible though that was, there was something more horrible still – horrible, that was, on awakening, for in the dream it seemed perfectly natural and inevitable. *She, Alix Martin, was glad that her husband was dead*; she stretched out grateful hands to the murderer, sometimes she thanked him. The dream always ended the same way, with herself clasped in Dick Windyford's arms.

She had said nothing of this dream to her husband, but secretly it had perturbed her more than she liked to admit. Was it a warning – a warning against Dick Windyford?

Alix was roused from her thoughts by the sharp ringing of the telephone bell from within the house. She entered the cottage and picked up the receiver. Suddenly she swayed, and put out a hand against the wall.

'Who did you say was speaking?'

'Why, Alix, what's the matter with your voice? I wouldn't have known it. It's Dick.'

'Oh!' said Alix. 'Oh! Where – where are you?'

'At the *Traveller's Arms* – that's the right name, isn't it? Or don't you even know of the existence of your village pub? I'm on my holiday – doing a bit of fishing here. Any objections to my looking you two good people up this evening after dinner?'

'No,' said Alix sharply. 'You mustn't come.'

There was a pause, and then Dick's voice, with a subtle alteration in it, spoke again.

'I beg your pardon,' he said formally. 'Of course I won't bother you—'

Alix broke in hastily. He must think her behaviour too extraordinary. It *was* extraordinary. Her nerves must be all to pieces.

'I only meant that we were – engaged tonight,' she explained, trying to make her voice sound as natural as possible. 'Won't you – won't you come to dinner tomorrow night?'

But Dick obviously noted the lack of cordiality in her tone.

'Thanks very much,' he said, in the same formal voice, 'but I may be moving on any time. Depends if a pal of mine turns up or not. Good-bye Alix.' He paused, and then added hastily, in a different tone: 'Best of luck to you, my dear.'

Alix hung up the receiver with a feeling of relief.

'He mustn't come here,' she repeated to herself. 'He mustn't come here. Oh, what a fool I am! To imagine myself into a state like this. All the same, I'm glad he's not coming.'

She caught up a rustic rush hat from a table, and passed out into the garden again, pausing to look up at the name carved over the porch: Philomel Cottage.

'Isn't it a very fanciful name?' she had said to Gerald once before they were married. He had laughed.

'You little Cockney,' he had said affectionately. 'I don't believe you have ever heard a nightingale. I'm glad you haven't. Nightingales should sing only for lovers. We'll hear them together on a summer's evening outside our own home.'

And at the remembrance of how they had indeed heard them, Alix, standing in the doorway of her home, blushed happily.

It was Gerald who had found Philomel Cottage. He had come to Alix bursting with excitement. He had found the very spot for them – unique – a gem – the chance of a lifetime. And when Alix had seen it she too was captivated. It was true that the situation was rather lonely – they were two miles from the nearest village – but the cottage itself was so exquisite, with its old-world appearance and its solid comfort of bathrooms, hot water system, electric light, and telephone, that she fell a victim to its charm immediately. And then a hitch occurred. The owner, a rich man who had made it his whim, declined to let it. He would only sell.

Gerald Martin, though possessed of a good income, was unable to touch his capital. He could raise at most a thousand pounds. The owner was asking three. But Alix, who had set her heart on the place, came to the rescue. Her own capital was easily realized, being in bearer bonds. She would contribute half of it to the purchase of the home. So Philomel Cottage became their very own, and never for a minute had Alix regretted the choice. It was true that servants did not appreciate the rural solitude – indeed, at the moment they had none at all – but Alix, who had been starved of domestic life, thoroughly enjoyed cooking dainty little meals and looking after the house.

The garden, which was magnificently stocked with flowers, was attended by an old man from the village who came twice a week.

As she rounded the corner of the house, Alix was surprised to see the old gardener in question busy over the flower beds. She was surprised because his days for work were Mondays and Fridays, and today was Wednesday.

'Why, George, what are you doing here?' she asked, as she came towards him.

The old man straightened up with a chuckle, touching the brim of an aged cap.

'I thought as how you'd be surprised, ma'am. But 'tis this way. There be a fête over to Squire's on Friday, and I sez to myself, I sez, neither Mr Martin nor yet his good lady won't take it amiss if I comes for once on a Wednesday instead of a Friday.'

'That's quite all right,' said Alix. 'I hope you'll enjoy yourself at the fête.'

'I reckon to,' said George simply. 'It's a fine thing to be able to eat your fill and know all the time as it's not you as is paying for it. Squire allus has a proper sit-down tea for 'is tenants. Then I thought too, ma'am, as I might as well see you before you goes away so as to learn your wishes for the borders. You'll have no idea when you'll be back, ma'am, I suppose.'

'But I'm not going away.'

George stared at her.

'Bain't you going to Lunnon tomorrow?'

'No. What put such an idea into your head?'

George jerked his head over his shoulder.

'Met maister down to village yesterday. He told me you was

both going away to Lunnon tomorrow, and it was uncertain when you'd be back again.

'Nonsense,' said Alix, laughing. 'You must have misunderstood him.'

All the same, she wondered exactly what it could have been that Gerald had said to lead the old man into such a curious mistake. Going to London? She never wanted to see London again.

'I hate London,' she said suddenly and harshly.

'Ah!' said George placidly. 'I must have been mistook somehow, and yet he said it plain enough, it seemed to me. I'm glad you're stopping on here. I don't hold with all this gallivanting about, and I don't think nothing of Lunnon. I've never needed to go there. Too many moty cars – that's the trouble nowadays. Once people have got a moty car, blessed if they can stay still anywheres. Mr Ames, wot used to have this house – nice, peaceable sort of gentleman he was until he bought one of them things. Hadn't had it a month before he put up this cottage for sale. A tidy lot he spent on it, too, with taps in all the bedrooms, and the electric light and all. "You'll never see your money back," I sez to him. "But," he sez to me, "I'll get every penny of two thousand pounds for this house." And sure enough, he did.'

'He got three thousand,' said Alix, smiling.

'Two thousand,' repeated George. 'The sum he was asking was talked of at the time.'

'It really was three thousand,' said Alix.

'Ladies never understand figures,' said George, unconvinced. 'You'll not tell me that Mr Ames had the face to stand up to you, and say three thousand brazen-like in a loud voice?'

'He didn't say it to me,' said Alix; 'he said it to my husband.'

George stooped again to his flower bed.

'The price was two thousand,' he said obstinately.

Alix did not trouble to argue with him. Moving to one of the further beds, she began to pick an armful of flowers.

As she moved with her fragrant posy towards the house, Alix

noticed a small, dark-green object peeping from between some leaves in one of the beds. She stopped and picked it up, recognizing it for her husband's pocket diary.

She opened it, scanning the entries with some amusement. Almost from the beginning of their married life she had realized that the impulsive and emotional Gerald had the uncharacteristic virtues of neatness and method. He was extremely fussy about meals being punctual, and always planned his day ahead with the accuracy of a time-table.

Looking through the diary, she was amused to notice the entry on the date of 14th May: 'Marry Alix St Peter's 2.30.'

'The big silly,' murmured Alix to herself, turning the pages. Suddenly she stopped.

' "Wednesday, 18th June" – why, that's today.'

In the space for that day was written in Gerald's neat, precise hand: '9 p.m.' Nothing else. What had Gerald planned to do at 9 p.m.? Alix wondered. She smiled to herself as she realized that had this been a story, like those she had so often read, the diary would doubtless have furnished her with some sensational revelation. It would have had in it for certain the name of another woman. She fluttered the back pages idly. There were dates, appointments, cryptic references to business deals, but only one woman's name – her own.

Yet as she slipped the book into her pocket and went on with her flowers to the house, she was aware of a vague uneasiness. Those words of Dick Windyford's recurred to her almost as though he had been at her elbow repeating them: 'The man's a perfect stranger to you. You know nothing about him.'

It was true. What did she know about him? After all, Gerald was forty. In forty years there must have been women in his life . . .

Alix shook herself impatiently. She must not give way to these thoughts. She had a far more instant preoccupation to deal with. Should she, or should she not, tell her husband that Dick Windyford had rung her up?

There was the possibility to be considered that Gerald might have already run across him in the village. But in that case he would be sure to mention it to her immediately upon his return, and matters would be taken out of her hands. Otherwise – what? Alix was aware of a distinct desire to say nothing about it.

If she told him, he was sure to suggest asking Dick Windyford to Philomel Cottage. Then she would have to explain that Dick had proposed himself, and that she had made an excuse to prevent his coming. And when he asked her why she had done so, what could she say? Tell him her dreams? But he would only laugh – or, worse, see that she attached an importance to it which he did not.

In the end, rather shamefacedly, Alix decided to say nothing. It was the first secret she had ever kept from her husband, and the consciousness of it made her feel ill at ease.

When she heard Gerald returning from the village shortly before lunch, she hurried into the kitchen and pretended to be busy with the cooking so as to hide her confusion.

It was evident at once that Gerald had seen nothing of Dick Windyford. Alix felt at once relieved and embarrassed. She was definitely committed now to a policy of concealment.

It was not until after their simple evening meal, when they were sitting in the oak-beamed living-room with the windows thrown open to let in the sweet night air scented with the perfume of the mauve and white stocks outside, that Alix remembered the pocket diary.

'Here's something you've been watering the flowers with,' she said, and threw it into his lap.

'Dropped it in the border, did I?'

'Yes; I know all your secrets now.'

'Not guilty,' said Gerald, shaking his head.

'What about your assignation at nine o'clock tonight?'

'Oh, that—' He seemed taken aback for a moment, then he smiled as though something afforded him particular amusement. 'It's an assignation with a particularly nice girl, Alix. She's got brown hair and blue eyes and she's very like you.'

'I don't understand,' said Alix, with mock severity. 'You're evading the point.'

'No, I'm not. As a matter of fact, that's a reminder that I'm going to develop some negatives tonight, and I want you to help me.'

Gerald Martin was an enthusiastic photographer. He had a somewhat old-fashioned camera, but with an excellent lens, and he developed his own plates in a small cellar which he had had fitted up as a dark room.

'And it must be done at nine o'clock precisely,' said Alix teasingly.

Gerald looked a little vexed.

'My dear girl,' he said, with a shade of testiness in his manner, 'one should always plan a thing for a definite time. Then one gets through one's work properly.'

Alix sat for a minute or two in silence, watching her husband as he lay in his chair smoking, his dark head flung back and the clear-cut lines of his clean-shaven face showing up against the sombre background. And suddenly, from some unknown source, a wave of panic surged over her, so that she cried out before she could stop herself: 'Oh, Gerald, I wish I knew more about you!'

Her husband turned an astonished face upon her.

'But, my dear Alix, you do know all about me. I've told you of my boyhood in Northumberland, of my life in South Africa, and these last ten years in Canada which have brought me success.'

'Oh! business!' said Alix scornfully.

Gerald laughed suddenly.

'I know what you mean – love affairs. You women are all the same. Nothing interests you but the personal element.'

Alix felt her throat go dry, as she muttered indistinctly: 'Well, but there must have been – love affairs. I mean – if I only knew—'

There was silence again for a minute or two. Gerald Martin was frowing, a look of indecision on his face. When he spoke it was gravely, without a trace of his former bantering manner.

'Do you think it wise, Alix, this – Bluebeard's chamber business? There have been women in my life; yes, I don't deny it. You wouldn't believe me if I did deny it. But I can swear to you truthfully that not one of them meant anything to me.'

There was a ring of sincerity in his voice which comforted the listening wife.

'Satisfied, Alix?' he asked with a smile. Then he looked at her with a shade of curiousity.

'What has turned your mind on to these unpleasant subjects tonight of all nights?'

Alix got up and began to walk about restlessly.

'Oh, I don't know,' she said. 'I've been nervy all day.'

'That's odd,' said Gerald, in a low voice, as though speaking to himself. 'That's very odd.'

'Why is it odd?'

'Oh, my dear girl, don't flash out at me so. I only said it was odd because as a rule you're so sweet and serene.'

Alix forced a smile.

'Everything's conspired to annoy me today,' she confessed. 'Even old George had got some ridiculous idea into his head that we were going away to London. he said you had told him so.'

'Where did you see him?' asked Gerald sharply.

'He came to work today instead of Friday.'

'Damned old fool,' said Gerald angrily.

Alix stared in surprise. Her husband's face was convulsed with rage. She had never seen him so angry. Seeing her astonishment Gerald made an effort to regain control of himself.

'Well, he is a damned old fool,' he protested.

'What can you have said to make him think that?'

'I? I never said anything. At least – oh, yes, I remember; I made some weak joke about being "off to London in the morning," and I suppose he took it seriously. Or else he didn't hear properly. You undeceived him, of course?'

He waited anxiously for her reply.

'Of course, but he's the sort of old man who if once he gets an idea in his head – well, it isn't easy to get it out again.'

Then she told him of George's insistence on the sum asked for the cottage.

Gerald was silent for a minute or two, then he said slowly:

'Ames was willing to take two thousand in cash and the

remaining thousand on mortgage. That's the origin of that mistake, I fancy.'

'Very likely,' agreed Alix.

Then she looked up at the clock, and pointed to it with a mischievous finger.

'We ought to be getting down to it, Gerald. Five minutes behind schedule.'

A very peculiar smile came over Gerald Martin's face.

'I've changed my mind,' he said quietly; 'I shan't do any photography tonight.'

A woman's mind is a curious thing. When she went to bed that Wednesday night Alix's mind was contented and at rest. Her momentarily assailed happiness reasserted itself, triumphant as of yore.

But by the evening of the following day she realized that some subtle forces were at work undermining it. Dick Windyford had not rung up again, nevertheless she felt what she supposed to be his influence at work. Again and again those words of his recurred to her: '*The man's a perfect stranger. You know nothing about him.*' And with them came the memory of her husband's face, photographed clearly on her brain, as he said: 'Do you think it wise, Alix, this – Bluebeard's chamber business?' Why had he said that.

There had been warning in them – a hint of menace. It was as though he had said in effect: 'You had better not pry into my life, Alix. You may get a nasty shock if you do.'

By Friday morning Alix had convinced herself that there *had* been a woman in Gerald's life – a Bluebeard's chamber that he had sedulously sought to conceal from her. Her jealousy, slow to awaken, was now rampant.

Was it a woman he had been going to meet that night at 9 p.m.? Was his story of photographs to develop a lie invented upon the spur of the moment?

Three days ago she would have sworn that she knew her husband through and through. Now it seemed to her that he was a stranger of whom she knew nothing. She remembered his unreasonable anger against old George, so at variance with his usual good-tempered manner. A small thing, perhaps, but it showed her that she did not really know the man who was her husband.

There were several little things required on Friday from the village. In the afternoon Alix suggested that she should go for them whilst Gerald remained in the garden; but somewhat to her surprise he opposed this plan vehemently, and insisted on going himself whilst she remained at home. Alix was forced to give way to him, but his insistence surprised and alarmed her. Why was he so anxious to prevent her going to the village?

Suddenly an explanation suggested itself to her which made the whole thing clear. Was it not possible that, whilst saying nothing to her, Gerald had indeed come across Dick Windyford? Her own jealousy, entirely dormant at the time of their marriage, had only developed afterwards. Might it not be the same with Gerald? Might he not be anxious to prevent her seeing Dick Windyford again? This explanation was so consistent with the facts, and so comforting to Alix's perturbed mind, that she embraced it eagerly.

Yet when tea-time had come and passed she was restless and ill at ease. She was struggling with a temptation that had assailed her ever since Gerald's departure. Finally, pacifying her conscience with the assurance that the room did need a thorough tidying, she went upstairs to her husband's dressing-room. She took a duster with her to keep up the pretence of housewifery.

'If I were only sure,' she repeated to herself. 'If I could only be *sure.*'

In vain she told herself that anything compromising would have been destroyed ages ago. Against that she argued that men do sometimes keep the most damning piece of evidence through an exaggerated sentimentality.

In the end Alix succumbed. Her cheeks burning with the shame of her action, she hunted breathlessly through packets of letters and documents, turned out the drawers, even went through the pockets of her husband's clothes. Only two drawers eluded her: the lower drawer of the chest of drawers and the small right-hand drawer of the writing-desk were both locked. But Alix was by now lost to all shame. In one of those drawers she was convinced that she would find evidence of this imaginary woman of the past who obsessed her.

She remembered that Gerald had left his keys lying carelessly on the sideboard downstairs. She fetched them and tried them one by one. The third key fitted the writing-table drawer. Alix pulled it open eagerly. There was a cheque-book and a wallet stuffed with notes, and at the back of the drawer a packet of letters tied up with a piece of tape.

Her breath coming unevenly, Alix untied the tape. Then a deep, burning blush overspread her face, and she dropped the letters back into the drawer, closing and relocking it. For the letters were her own, written to Gerald Martin before she married him.

She turned now to the chest of drawers, more with a wish to feel that she had left nothing undone than from any expectation of finding what she sought.

To her annoyance none of the keys on Gerald's bunch fitted the drawer in question. Not to be defeated, Alix went into the other rooms and brought back a selection of keys with her. To her satisfaction the key of the spare room wardrobe also fitted the chest of drawers. But there was nothing in it but a roll of newspaper clippings already dirty and discoloured with age.

Alix breathed a sigh of relief. Nevertheless, she glanced at the clippings, curious to know what subject had interested Gerald so much that he had taken the trouble to keep the dusty roll. They were nearly all American papers, dated some seven years ago, and dealing with the trial of the notorious swindler and bigamist, Charles Lemaitre. Lemaitre had been suspected of doing away with his women victims. A skeleton had been found beneath the floor of one of the houses he had rented, and most of the women he had 'married' had never been heard of again.

He had defended himself from the charge with consummate skill, aided by some of the best legal talent in the United States. The Scottish verdict of 'Not Proven' might perhaps have stated the case best. In its absence, he was found Not Guilty on the capital charge, though sentenced to a long term of imprisonment on the other charges preferred against him.

Alix remembered the excitement caused by the case at the time, and also the sensation aroused by the escape of Lemaitre some three years later. He had never been recaptured. The personality of the man and his extraordinary power over women had been discussed at great length in the English papers at the time, together with an account of his excitability in court, his passionate protestations, and his occasional sudden physical collapses, due to the fact that he had a weak heart, though the ignorant accredited it to his dramatic powers.

There was a picture of him in one of the clippings Alix held, and she studied it with some interest – a long-bearded, scholarly looking gentleman.

Who was it the face reminded her of? Suddenly, with a shock, she realized that it was Gerald himself. The eyes and brow bore a strong resemblance to his. Perhaps he had kept the cutting for that reason. Her eyes went on to the paragraph beside the picture. Certain dates, it seemed, had been entered in the accused's pocket-book, and it was contended that these were dates when he had done away with his victims. Then a woman gave evidence and identified the prisoner positively by the fact that he had a mole on his left wrist, just below the palm of the hand.

Alix dropped the papers and swayed as she stood. *On his left wrist, just below the palm, her husband had a small scar.*

The room whirled round her. Afterwards it struck her as strange that she should have leaped at once to such absolute certainty. Gerald Martin was Charles Lemaitre! She knew it, and accepted it in a flash. Disjointed fragments whirled through her brain, like pieces of a jig-saw puzzle fitting into place.

The money paid for the house – her money – her money only; the bearer bonds she had entrusted to his keeping. Even her dream appeared in its true significance. Deep down in her, her subconscious self had always feared Gerald Martin and wished to escape from him. And it was to Dick Windyford this self of hers had looked for help. That, too, was why she was able to accept the truth so easily, without doubt or hesitation. She was to have been another of Lemaitre's victims. Very soon, perhaps . . .

A half-cry escaped her as she remembered something. *Wednesday 9 p.m.* The cellar, with the flagstones that were so easily raised! Once before he had buried one of his victims in a cellar. It had been all planned for Wednesday night. But to write it down beforehand in that methodical manner – insanity! No, it was logical. Gerald always made a memorandum of his engagements: murder was to him a business proposition like any other.

But what had saved her? What could possibly have saved her? Had he relented at the last minute? No. In a flash the answer came to her – *old George.*

She understood now her husband's uncontrollable anger. Doubtless he had paved the way by telling everyone he met that they were going to London the next day. Then George had come to work unexpectedly, had mentioned London to her, and she had contradicted the story. Too risky to do away with her that night, with old George repeating that conversation. But what an escape! If she had not happened to mention that trivial matter – Alix shuddered.

But there was no time to be lost. She must get away at once – before he came back. She hurriedly replaced the roll of clippings in the drawer, shut it, and locked it.

And then she stayed motionless as though frozen to stone. She heard the creak of the gate into the road. *Her husband had returned.*

For a moment Alix stayed as though petrified, then she crept on tiptoe to the window, looking out from behind the shelter of the curtain.

Yes, it was her husband. He was smiling to himself and humming a little tune. In his hand he held an object which almost made the terrified girl's heart stop beating. It was a brand-new spade.

Alix leaped to a knowledge born of instinct. *It was to be to-night.*

But there was still a chance. Gerald, humming his little tune, went round to the back of the house.

Without hesitating a moment, she ran down the stairs and out of the cottage. But just as she emerged from the door, her husband came round the other side of the house.

'Hallo,' he said, 'where are you running off to in such a hurry?'

Alix strove desperately to appear calm and as usual. Her chance was gone for the moment, but if she was careful not to arouse his suspicions, it would come again later. Even now, perhaps . . .

'I was going to walk to the end of the lane and back,' she said in a voice that sounded weak and uncertain to her own ears.

'Right,' said Gerald. 'I'll come with you.'

'No – please, Gerald. I'm – nervy, headachy – I'd rather go alone.'

He looked at her attentively. She fancied a momentary suspicion gleamed in his eye.

'What's the matter with you, Alix? You're pale – trembling.'

'Nothing.' She forced herself to be brusque – smiling. 'I've got a headache, that's all. A walk will do me good.'

'Well, it's no good your saying you don't want me,' declared Gerald, with his easy laugh. 'I'm coming, whether you want me or not.'

She dared not protest further. If he suspected that she *knew* . . .

With an effort she managed to regain something of her normal manner. Yet she had an uneasy feeling that he looked at her sideways every now and then, as though not quite satisfied. She felt that his suspicions were not completely allayed.

When they returned to the house he insisted on her lying down, and brought some eau-de-Cologne to bathe her temples. He was, as ever, the devoted husband. Alix felt herself as helpless as though bound hand and foot in a trap.

Not for a minute would he leave her alone. He went with her into the kitchen and helped her to bring in the simple cold dishes she had already prepared. Supper was a meal that choked her, yet she forced herself to eat, and even to appear gay and natural. She knew now that she was fighting for her life. She was alone with this man, miles from help, absolutely at his mercy. Her only chance was so to lull his suspicions that he would leave her alone for a few minutes – long enough for her to get to the telephone in the hall and summon assistance. That was her only hope now.

A momentary hope flashed over her as she remembered how he had abandoned his plan before. Suppose she told him that Dick Windyford was coming up to see them that evening?

The words trembled on her lips – then she rejected them hastily. This man would not be baulked a second time. There was a determination, an elation, underneath his calm bearing that sickened her. She would only precipitate the crime. He would murder her there and then, and calmly ring up Dick Windyford with a tale of having been suddenly called away. Oh! If only Dick Windyford were coming to the house this evening! If Dick . . .

A sudden idea flashed into her mind. She looked sharply sideways at her husband as though she feared that he might read her mind. With the forming of a plan, her courage was reinforced. She became so completely natural in manner that she marvelled at herself.

She made the coffee and took it out to the porch where they often sat on fine evenings.

'By the way,' said Gerald suddenly, 'we'll do those photographs later.'

Alix felt a shiver run through her, but she replied, nonchalantly: 'Can't you manage alone? I'm rather tired tonight.'

'It won't take long.' He smiled to himself. 'And I can promise you you won't be tired afterwards.'

The words seemed to amuse him. Alix shuddered. Now or never was the time to carry out her plan.

She rose to her feet.

'I'm just going to telephone to the butcher,' she announced nonchalantly. 'Don't you bother to move.'

'To the butcher? At this time of night?'

'His shop's shut, of course, silly. But he's in his house all right. And tomorrow's Saturday, and I want him to bring me some veal cutlets early, before someone else grabs them off him. The old dear will do anything for me.'

She passed quickly into the house, closing the door behind her. She heard Gerald say: 'Don't shut the door,' and was quick with her light reply: 'It keeps the moths out. I hate moths. Are you afraid I'm going to make love to the butcher, silly?'

Once inside, she snatched down the telephone receiver and gave the number of the *Traveller's Arms*. She was put through at once.

'Mr Windyford? Is he still there? Can I speak to him?'

Then her heart gave a sickening thump. The door was pushed open and her husband came into the hall.

'Do go away, Gerald,' she said pettishly. 'I hate any one listening when I'm telephoning.'

He merely laughed and threw himself into a chair.

'Sure it really is the butcher you're telephoning to?' he quizzed.

Alix was in despair. Her plan had failed. In a minute Dick Windyford would come to the phone. Should she risk all and cry out an appeal for help?

And then, as she nervously depressed and released the little key in the receiver she was holding, which permits the voice to be heard or not heard at the other end, another plan flashed into her head.

'It will be difficult,' she thought to herself. 'It means keeping my head, and thinking of the right words, and not faltering for a moment, but I believe I could do it. I *must* do it.'

And at that minute she heard Dick Windyford's voice at the other end of the 'phone.

Alix drew a deep breath. Then she depressed the key firmly and spoke.

'*Mrs Martin speaking – from Philomel Cottage. Please come* (she released the key) tomorrow morning with six nice veal cutlets (she depressed the key again). *It's very important* (she released the key). Thank you so much, Mr Hexworthy; you don't mind my ringing you up so late, I hope, but those veal cutlets are really a matter of (she depressed the key again) *life or death* (she released it). Very well – tomorrow morning (she depressed it) *as soon as possible.*

She replaced the receiver on the hook and turned to face her husband, breathing hard.

'So that's how you talk to your butcher, is it?' said Gerald.

'It's the feminine touch,' said Alix lightly.

She was simmering with excitement. He had suspected nothing. Dick, even if he didn't understand, would come.

She passed into the sitting-room and switched on the electric light. Gerald followed her.

'You seem very full of spirits now?' he said, watching her curiously.

'Yes,' said Alix. 'My headache's gone.'

She sat down in her usual seat and smiled at her husband as he sank into his own chair opposite her. She was saved. It was only five-and-twenty past eight. Long before nine o'clock Dick would have arrived.

'I didn't think much of that coffee you gave me,' complained Gerald. 'It tasted very bitter.'

'It's a new kind I was trying. We won't have it again if you don't like it, dear.'

Alix took up a piece of needlework and began to stitch. Gerald read a few pages of his book. Then he glanced up at the clock and tossed the book away.

'Half-past eight. Time to go down to the cellar and start work.'

The sewing slipped from Alix's fingers.

'Oh, not yet. Let us wait until nine o'clock.'

'No, my girl – half-past eight. That's the time I fixed. You'll be able to get to bed all the earlier.'

'But I'd rather wait until nine.'

'You know when I fix a time, I always stick to it. Come along, Alix. I'm not going to wait a minute longer.'

Alix looked up at him, and in spite of herself she felt a wave of terror slide over her. The mask had been lifted. Gerald's hands

99

were twitching, his eyes were shining with excitement, he was continually passing his tongue over his dry lips. He no longer cared to conceal his excitement.

Alix thought: 'It's true – *he can't wait* – he's like a madman.'

He strode over to her, and jerked her to her feet with a hand on her shoulder.

'Come on, my girl – or I'll carry you there.'

His tone was gay, but there was an undisguised ferocity behind it that appalled her. With a supreme effort she jerked herself free and clung cowering against the wall. She was powerless. She couldn't get away – she couldn't do anything – and he was coming towards her.

'Now, Alix—'

'No – no.'

She screamed, her hands held out impotently to ward him off.

'Gerald – stop – I've got something to tell you, something to confess—'

He did stop.

'To confess?' he said curiously.

'Yes, to confess.' She had used the words at random, but she went on desperately, seeking to hold his arrested attention.

A look of contempt swept over his face.

'A former lover, I suppose,' he sneered.

'No,' said Alix. 'Something else. You'd call it, I expect – yes, you'd call it a crime.'

And at once she saw that she had struck the right note. Again his attention was arrested, held. Seeing that, her nerve came back to her. She felt mistress of the situation once more.

'You had better sit down again,' she said quietly.

She herself crossed the room to her old chair and sat down. She even stooped and picked up her needlework. But behind her calmness she was thinking and inventing feverishly; for the story she invented must hold his interest until help arrived.

'I told you,' she said slowly, 'that I had been a shorthand-typist for fifteen years. That was not entirely true. There were two intervals. The first occurred when I was twenty-two. I came across a man, an elderly man with a little property. He fell in love with me and asked me to marry him. I accepted. We were married.' She paused. 'I induced him to insure his life in my favour.'

She saw a sudden keen interest spring up in her husband's face, and went on with renewed assurance:

'During the war I worked for a time in a hospital dispensary. There I had the handling of all kinds of rare drugs and poisons.'

She paused reflectively. He was keenly interested now, not a doubt of it. The murderer is bound to have an interest in murder. She had gambled on that, and succeeded. She stole a glance at the clock. It was five-and-twenty to nine.

'There is one poison – it is a little white powder. A pinch of it means death. You know something about poisons, perhaps?'

She put the question in some trepidation. If he did, she would have to be careful.

'No,' said Gerald; 'I know very little about them.'

She drew a breath of relief.

'You have heard of hyosine, of course? This is a drug that acts much the same way, but is absolutely untraceable. Any doctor would give a certificate of heart failure. I stole a small quantity of this drug and kept it by me.'

She paused, marshalling her forces.

'Go on,' said Gerald.

'No. I'm afraid. I can't tell you. Another time.'

'Now,' he said impatiently. 'I want to hear.'

'We had been married a month. I was very good to my elderly husband, very kind and devoted. He spoke in praise of me to all the neighbours. Every one knew what a devoted wife I was. I always made his coffee myself every evening. One evening, when we were alone together, I put a pinch of the deadly alkaloid in his cup—'

Alix paused, and carefully re-threaded her needle. She, who had never acted in her life, rivalled the greatest actress in the world at this moment. She was actually living the part of the cold-blooded poisoner.

'It was very peaceful. I sat watching him. Once he gasped a little and asked for air. I opened the window. Then he said he could not move from his chair. *Presently he died.*'

She stopped smiling. It was a quarter to nine. Surely they would come soon.

'How much,' said Gerald, 'was the insurance money?'

'About two thousand pounds. I speculated with it, and lost it. I went back to my office work. But I never meant to remain there long. Then I met another man. I had stuck to my maiden name at the office. He didn't know I had been married before. He was a younger man, rather good-looking, and quite well off. We were married quietly in Sussex. He didn't want to insure his life, but of course he made a will in my favour. He liked me to make his coffee myself just as my first husband had done.'

Alix smiled reflectively, and added simply: 'I make very good coffee.'

Then she went on:

'I had several friends in the village where we were living. They were very sorry for me, with my husband dying suddenly of heart failure one evening after dinner. I didn't quite like the doctor. I don't think he suspected me, but he was certainly very surprised at my husband's sudden death. I don't quite know why I drifted back to the office again. Habit, I suppose. My second husband left about four thousand pounds. I didn't speculate with it this time; I invested it. Then, you see—'

But she was interrupted. Gerald Martin, his face suffused with blood, half-choking, was pointing a shaking forefinger at her.

'The coffee – my God! the coffee!'

She stared at him.

'I understand now why it was so bitter. You devil. You've been up to your tricks again.'

His hands gripped the arms of his chair. He was ready to spring upon her.

'You've poisoned me.'

Alix had retreated from him to the fire-place. Now, terrified, she opened her lips to deny – and then paused. In another minute he would spring upon her. She summoned all her strength. Her eyes held his steadily, compellingly.

'Yes,' she said. 'I poisoned you. Already the poison is working.

At this minute you can't move from your chair – you can't move—'

If she could keep him there – even a few minutes. . .

Ah! what was that? Footsteps on the road. The creak of the gate. Then footsteps on the path outside. The outer door opening.

'*You can't move,*' she said again.

Then she slipped past him and fled headlong from the room to fall fainting into Dick Windyford's arms.

'My God! Alix!' he cried.

Then he turned to the man with him, a tall, stalwart figure in policeman's uniform.

'Go and see what's been happening in that room.'

He laid Alix carefully down on a couch and bent over her.

'My little girl,' he murmured. 'My poor little girl. What have they been doing to you?'

Her eyelids fluttered and her lips just murmured his name.

Dick was aroused by the policeman's touching him on the arm.

'There's nothing in that room, sir, but a man sitting in a chair. Looks as though he'd had some kind of bad fright, and—'

'Yes?'

'Well, sir, he's – dead.'

They were startled by hearing Alix's voice. She spoke as though in some kind of dream, her eyes still closed.

'*And presently,*' she said, almost as though she were quoting from something, '*he died*—'

A Pair of Yellow Lilies

Ruth Rendell

A famous designer, young still, who first became well known when she made a princess's wedding dress, was coming to speak to the women's group of which Bridget Thomas was secretary. She would be the second speaker in the autumn program, which was devoted to success and how women had achieved it. Repeated requests on Bridget's part for a biography from Annie Carter so that she could provide her members with interesting background information had met with no response. Bridget had even begun to wonder if she would remember to come and give her talk in three weeks' time. Meanwhile, obliged to do her own research, she had gone into the public library to look Annie Carter up in *Who's Who*.

Bridget had a precarious job in a small and not very prosperous bookshop. In her mid-thirties, with a rather pretty face that often looked worried and worn, she thought that she might learn something from this current series of talks. Secrets of success might be imparted, blueprints for achievements, even shortcuts to prosperity. She never had enough money, never knew security, could not have dreamed of aspiring to an Annie Carter ready-to-wear even when such a garment had been twice marked down in a sale. Clothes, anyway, were hardly a priority, coming a long way down the list of essentials which was headed by rent, fares, and food, in that order.

In the library she was not noticeable. She was not, in any case and anywhere, the kind of woman on whom second glances were bestowed. On this Wednesday evening, when the shop closed at its normal time and the library later than usual, she could be seen by those few who cared to look wearing a long black skirt with a dusty appearance, a T-shirt of a slightly different shade of black – it had been washed fifty times at least – and a waistcoat in dark striped cotton. Her shoes were black-velvet Chinese slippers with instep straps and there was a hole she didn't know about in her turquoise-blue tights, low down on the left calf. Bridget's hair was wispy, long and fair, worn in loops. She was carrying an enormous black-leather bag, capacious and heavy, and full of unnecessary things. Herself the first to admit this, she often said she meant to make changes in the matter of this bag but she never got around to it.

This evening the bag contained a number of crumpled tissues, some pink, some white, a spray bottle of Wild Musk cologne, three ballpoint pens, a pair of nail scissors, a pair of nail clippers, a London tube pass, a British Telecom phone-card, an address book, a mascara wand in a shade called After-Midnight Blue, a chequebook, a notebook, a postcard from a friend on holiday in Brittany, a calculator, a paperback of Vasari's *Lives of the Artists*, which Bridget had always meant to read but was not getting on very fast with, a container of nasal spray, a bunch of keys, a book of matches, a silver ring with a green stone, probably onyx, a pheasant's feather picked up while staying for the weekend in someone's cottage in Somerset, three quarters of a bar of milk chocolate, a pair of sunglasses, and her wallet – which contained the single credit card she possessed, her bank-cheque card, her library card, her never-needed driving licence, and seventy pounds, give or take a little, in five- and ten-pound notes. There was also about four pounds in change.

On the previous evening, Bridget had been to see her aunt. This was the reason for her carrying so much money. Bridget's Aunt Monica was an old woman who had never married and whom her brother, Bridget's father, referred to with brazen insensitivity as 'a maiden lady'. Bridget thought this outrageous and remonstrated with her father but was unable to bring him to see anything offensive in this expression. Though Monica had never had a husband, she had been successful in other areas of life, and might indeed almost have qualified to join Bridget's list of female achievers fit to speak to her women's group. Inherited-money wisely invested brought her in a substantial income, and this added to the pension derived from having been quite high up the ladder in the Civil Service made her nearly rich.

Bridget did not like taking Monica Thomas's money. Or she

told herself she didn't – actually meaning that she liked the money very much but felt humiliated, as a young healthy woman who ought to have been able to keep herself adequately, taking money from an old one who had done so and still did. Monica, not invariably during these visits but often enough, would ask her how she was managing.

'Making ends meet, are you?' was the form this inquiry usually took.

Bridget felt a little tide of excitement rising in her at these words because she knew they signified a coming munificence. She simultaneously felt ashamed at being excited by such a thing. This was the way, she believed, other women might feel at the prospect of lovemaking or discovering themselves pregnant or getting promotion. She felt excited because her old aunt, her maiden aunt tucked away in a gloomy flat in Fulham, was about to give her fifty pounds.

Characteristically, Monica prepared the ground. 'You may as well have it now instead of waiting till I'm gone.'

And Bridget would smile and look away – or, if she felt brave, tell her aunt not to talk about dying. Once she had gone so far as to say, 'I don't come here for the sake of what you give me, you know,' but as she put this into words she knew she did. And Monica, replying tartly, 'And I don't see my little gifts as paying you for your visits,' must have known that she did and they did, and that the two of them were involved in a commercial transaction, calculated enough, but imbrued with guilt and shame.

Bridget always felt that at her age, thirty-six, and her aunt's, seventy-two, it should be she who gave alms and her aunt who received them. That was the usual way of things. Here the order was reversed, and with a hand that she had to restrain forcibly from trembling with greed and need and excitement she had reached out on the previous evening for the notes that were presented as a sequel to another of Monica's favourite remarks, that she would like to see Bridget better dressed. With only a vague grasp of changes in the cost of living, Monica nevertheless knew that for any major changes in her niece's wardrobe to take place a larger than usual sum would be required and another twenty-five had been added to the customary fifty.

Five pounds or so had been spent during the course of the day. Bridget had plenty to do with the rest, which did not include buying the simple dark coat and skirt and pink twinset Monica had suggested. There was the gas bill, for instance, and the chance at last of settling the credit-card account, on which interest was being paid at twenty-one per cent. Not that Bridget had no wistful thoughts of beautiful things she would like to possess and most likely never would. A chair in a shop window in Bond Street, for instance, a chair which stood alone in slender, almost arrogant elegance, with its high-stepping legs and sweetly curved back, she imagined gracing her room as a bringer of daily renewed happiness and pride. Only today a woman had come into the shop to order the new Salman Rushdie and she had been wearing a dress that was unmistakably Annie Carter. Bridget had gazed at that dress as at some unattainable glory, at its bizarreries of zips round the sleeves and triangles excised from armpits, uneven hemline and slashed back, for if the truth were told it was the fantastic she admired in such matters and would not have been seen dead in a pink twinset.

She had gazed and longed, just as now, fetching *Who's Who* back to her seat at the table, she had stared in passing at the back of a glorious jacket. Afterwards, she could not have said if it was a man or woman wearing it, a person in jeans was all she could have guessed at. The person in jeans was pressed fairly close up against the science-fiction shelves, so that the back of the jacket, its most beautiful and striking area, was displayed to the best advantage. The jacket was made of blue denim with a design appliqued on it. Bridget knew the work was applique because she had learned something of this technique herself at a handicrafts class, all part of the horizon-widening, life-enhancing programme with which she combatted loneliness. Patches of satin and silk and brocade had been used in the work, and beads and sequins and gold threads as well. The design was of a flock of brilliant butterflies, purple and turquoise and vermilion and royal blue and fuchsia pink, tumbling and fluttering from the open mouths of a pair of yellow lilies. Bridget had gazed at this fantastic picture in silks and jewels and then looked quickly away, resolving to look no more, she desired so much to possess it herself.

Annie Carter's *Who's Who* entry mentioned a book she had written on fashion in the early Eighties. Bridget thought it would be sensible to acquaint herself with it. It would provide her with something to talk about when she and the committee entertained the designer to supper after her talk. Leaving *Who's Who* open on the table and her bag wedged between the table legs and the leg of her chair, Bridget went off to consult the library's computer as to whether the book was in stock.

Afterwards she recalled, though dimly, some of the people she had seen as she crossed the floor of the library to where the computer was. An old man in gravy-brown clothes reading a newspaper, two old women in fawn raincoats and pudding-basin hats, a child that ran about in defiance of its mother's threats and pleas. The mother was a woman about Bridget's own age, grossly fat, with fuzzy dark hair and swollen legs. There had been other people less memorable. The computer told her the book was in stock but out on loan. Bridget went back to her table and sat down. She read the sparse *Who's Who* entry once more, noting that Annie Carter's interests were bob-sleighing and collecting netsuke, which seemed to make her rather a daunting person, and then she reached down for her bag and the notebook it contained.

The bag had gone.

The feeling Bridget experienced is one everyone has when they lose something important or think they have lost it, the shock of loss. It was a physical sensation, as of something falling through her – turning over in her chest first and then tumbling down inside her body and out through the soles of her feet. She immediately told herself she couldn't have lost the bag, she couldn't have done, it couldn't have been stolen – who would have stolen it among that company? – she must have taken it with her to the computer. Bridget went back to the computer, she ran back, and the bag wasn't there. She told the two assistant librarians and then the librarian herself and they all looked round the library for the bag. It seemed to Bridget that by this time everyone else who had been in the library had swiftly disappeared – everyone, that is, but the old man reading the newspaper.

The librarian was extremely kind. They were about to close and she said she would go to the police with Bridget, it was on her way. Bridget continued to feel the shock of loss, sickening overturnings in her body and sensations of panic and disbelief. Her head seemed too lightly poised on her neck, almost as if it floated.

'It can't have happened,' she kept saying to the librarian. 'I just don't believe it could have happened in those few seconds I was away.'

'I'm afraid it did,' said the woman, who was too kind to say anything about Bridget's unwisdom in leaving the bag unattended even for a few seconds. 'It's nothing to do with me, but was there much money in it?'

'Quite a lot. Yes, quite a lot.' Bridget added humbly, 'Well, a lot for me.'

The police could offer very little hope of recovering the money. The bag, they said, and some of its contents might turn up. Meanwhile, Bridget had no means of getting into her room, no means even of phoning the credit-card company to notify them of the theft. The librarian, whose name was Elizabeth Derwent, saw to all that. She took Bridget to her own home and led her to the telephone and then took her to a locksmith. It was the beginning of what was to be an enduring friendship. Bridget might have lost so many of the most precious of her worldly goods, but as she said afterwards to her Aunt Monica, at least she got Elizabeth's friendship out of it.

'It's an ill wind that blows nobody any good,' said Monica, pressing fifty pounds in ten-pound notes into Bridget's hand.

But all this was in the future. That first evening, Bridget had to come to terms with the loss of seventy pounds, her driving licence, her credit card, her cheque book, the *Lives of the Artists* (she would never read it now), her address book, and the silver ring with the stone which was probably onyx. She mourned, alone there in her room. She fretted miserably, shock and disbelief having been succeeded by the inescapable certainty that someone had deliberately stolen her bag. Several cups of strong hot tea comforted her a little. Bridget had more in common with her aunt than she would have liked to think possible, being very much a latter-day maiden lady in every respect but maidenhood.

At the end of the week, a parcel came. It contained her wallet (empty but for the library card), the silver ring, her address book, her notebook, the nail scissors and the nail clippers, the mascara wand in the shade called After-Midnight Blue, and most of the things she had lost but for the money and the credit card and the cheque book, the driving licence, the paperback Vasari, and the bag itself. A letter accompanied the things. It said: 'Dear Miss Thomas, This name and address were in the notebook. I hope they are yours and that this will reach you. I found your things inside a plastic bag on top of a litter bin in Kensington Church Street. It was the wallet which made me think they were not things someone had meant to throw away. I am afraid this is absolutely all there was, though I have the feeling there was money in the wallet and other valuable things. Yours sincerely, Patrick Baker.'

His address and phone number headed the sheet of paper. Bridget, who was not usually impulsive, was so immediately brimming with amazed happiness and restored faith in human nature that she lifted the phone at once and dialled the number. He answered. It was a pleasant voice, educated, rather slow and deliberate in its enunciation of words, a young man's voice. She poured out her gratitude. How kind he was! What trouble he had been to! Not only to retrieve her things but to take them home, to parcel them up, pay the postage, stand in a queue no doubt at the post office! What could she do for him? How could she show the gratitude she felt?

Come and have a drink with him, he said. Well, of course she would, of course. She promised to have a drink with him and a place was arranged and a time, though she was already getting cold feet. She consulted Elizabeth.

'Having a drink in a pub in Kensington High Street couldn't do any harm,' said Elizabeth, smiling.

'It's not really something I do.' It wasn't something she had done for years, at any rate. In fact, it was two years since Bridget had even been out with a man, since her sad affair with the married accountant which had dragged on year after year before it finally came to an end. Drinking in pubs had not been a feature of the relationship. Sometimes they had made swift furtive love in the small office where clients' VAT files were kept. 'I suppose,' she said, 'it might make a pleasant change.'

The aspect of Patrick Baker which would have made him particularly attractive to most women, if it did not repel Bridget at least put her off. He was too good-looking for her. He was, in fact, radiantly beautiful, like an angel or a young Swedish tennis player. This, of course, did not specially matter that first time. But his looks registered with her as she walked across the little garden at the back of the pub and he rose from the table at which he was sitting. His looks frightened her and made her shy. It would not have been true, though, to say that she could not keep her eyes off him. Looking at him was altogether too much for her, it was almost an embarrassment, and she tried to keep her eyes turned away.

Nor would she have known what to say to him. Fortunately, he was eager to recount in detail his discovery of her property in the litter bin in Kensington Church Street. Bridget was good at listening and she listened. He told her also how he had once lost a briefcase in a tube train and a friend of his had had his wallet stolen on a train going from New York to Philadelphia. Emboldened by these homely and not at all sophisticated anecdotes, Bridget told him about the time her Aunt Monica had burglars and lost an emerald necklace which fortunately was insured. This prompted him to ask more about her aunt and Bridget found herself being quite amusing, recounting Monica's financial adventures. She didn't see why she shouldn't tell him the origins of the stolen money and he seemed interested when she said it came from Monica, who was in the habit of bestowing like sums on her.

'You see, she says I'm to have it one day – she means when she's dead, poor dear – so why not now?'

'Why not indeed?'

'It was just my luck to have my wallet stolen the day after she'd given me all that money.'

He asked her to have dinner with him. Bridget said all right, but it mustn't be anywhere expensive or grand. She asked Elizabeth what she should wear. There were in a clothes mood, for it was the evening of the Annie Carter talk to the women's group which Elizabeth had been persuaded to join.

'He doesn't dress at all formally himself,' Bridget said. 'Rather the reverse.' He and she had been out for another drink in the meantime. 'He was wearing this kind of safari suit with a purple shirt. But, oh, Elizabeth, he is amazing to look at. Rather too much so, if you know what I mean.'

Elizabeth didn't. She said that surely one couldn't be too goodlooking? Bridget said she knew she was being silly, but it embarrassed her a bit – well, being seen with him, if Elizabeth knew what she meant. It made her feel awkward.

'I'll lend you my black lace if you like,' Elizabeth said. 'It would suit you and it's suitable for absolutely everything.'

Bridget wouldn't borrow the black lace. She refused to sail in under anyone else's colours. She wouldn't borrow Aunt Monica's emerald necklace, either – the one she had bought to replace the necklace the burglars took. Her black skirt and the velvet top from the second hand shop in Hammersmith would be quite good enough. If she couldn't have an Annie Carter, she would rather not compromise. Monica, who naturally had never been told anything about the married accountant or his distant predecessor, the married primary-school teacher, spoke as if Patrick Baker were the first man Bridget had ever been alone with, and spoke too, as if marriage were a far from remote possibility. Bridget listened to all this while thinking how awful it would be if she were to fall in love with Patrick Baker and become addicted to his beauty and suffer when separated from him.

Even as she thought in this way, so prudently and with irony, she could see his face before her, its hawklike lineaments and its softnesses, the wonderful mouth and the large wide-set eyes, the hair that was fair and thick and the skin that was smooth and brown. She saw, too, his muscular figure, slender and graceful yet strong, his long hands and his tapering fingers, and she felt something long-suppressed, a prickle of desire that plucked very lightly at the inside of her and made her gasp a little.

The restaurant where they had their dinner was not grand or expensive, and this was just as well since at the end of the meal Patrick found that he had left his chequebook at home and Bridget was obliged to pay for their dinner out of the money Monica had given her to buy an evening dress. He was very grateful. He kissed her on the pavement outside the restaurant, or, if not quite outside it, under the archway that was the entrance to the mews. They went back to his place in a taxi.

He had quite a nice flat at the top of a house in Bayswater, not exactly overlooking the park but nearly. It was interesting what was happening to Bridget. Most of the time she was able to stand outside herself and view these deliberate acts of hers with detachment. She would have the pleasure of him, he was so beautiful, she would have it and that would be that. Such men were not for her, not at any rate for more than once or twice. But if she could once in a lifetime have one of them for once or twice, why not? Why not?

The life, too, the lifestyle, was not for her. On the whole, she was better off at home with a pot of strong hot tea and her embroidery or the latest paperback on changing attitudes to women in Western society. Nor had she any intention of sharing Aunt Monica's money when the time came. She had recently had to be stern with herself about a tendency, venal and degrading, to dream of that distant prospect when she would live in a World's End studio with a gallery, fit setting for the arrogant

Bond Street chair, and dress in a bold, eccentric manner, in flowing skirts and antique pelisses and fine old lace.

Going home with Patrick, she was rather drunk. Not drunk enough not to know what she was doing, but drunk enough not to care. She was drunk enough to shed her inhibitions while being sufficiently sober to know she had inhibitions, to know that they would be waiting to return to her quite unchanged. She went into Patrick's arms with delight, with the reckless abandon and determination to enjoy herself of someone embarking on a world cruise that must necessarily take place but once. Being in bed with him was not in the least like being in the VAT records office with the married accountant. She had known it would not be and that was why she was there. During the night the central heating went off, and failed, through some inadequacy of a fragile pilot light, to restart itself. It grew cold, but Bridget, in the arms of Patrick Baker, did not feel it.

She was the first to wake up. Bridget was the kind of person who is always the first to wake up. She lay in bed a little way apart from Patrick Baker and thought about what a lovely time she had had the night before and how that was enough and she would not see him again. Seeing him again might be dangerous and she could not afford, with her unmemorable appearance, her precarious job, and low wage, to put herself in peril. Presently she got up and said to Patrick, who had stirred a little and made an attempt in a kindly way to cuddle her, that she would make him a cup of tea.

Patrick put his nose out of the bedclothes and said it was freezing, the central heating had gone wrong, it was always going wrong. 'Don't get cold,' he said sleepily. 'Find something to put on in the cupboard.'

Even if they had been in the tropics, Bridget would not have dreamt of walking about a man's flat with no clothes on. She dressed. While the kettle was boiling, she looked with interest around Patrick's living room. There had been no opportunity to take any of it in on the previous evening. He was an untidy man, she noted, and his taste was not distinguished. You could see he bought his pictures ready-framed at Athena Art. He hadn't many books and most of what he had was science fiction, so it was rather a surprise to come upon Vasari's *Lives of the Artists* in paperback between a volume of fighting fantasy and a John Wyndham classic.

Perhaps she did, after all, feel cold. She was aware of a sudden unpleasant chill. It was comforting to feel the warmth of the kettle against her hands. She made the tea and took him a cup, setting it down on the bedside table, for he was fast asleep again. Shivering now, she opened the closet door and looked inside.

He seemed to possess a great many coats and jackets. She pushed the hangers along the rail, sliding tweed to brush against serge and linen against wild silk. His wardrobe was vast and complicated. He must have a great deal to spend on himself. The jacket with the butterflies slid into sudden brilliant view as if pushed there by some stage manager of fate. Everything conspired to make the sight of it dramatic, even the sun which came out and shed an unexpected ray into the open closet. Bridget gazed at the denim jacket as she had gazed with similar lust and wonder once before. She stared at the cascade of butterflies in purple and vermilion and turquoise, royal blue and fuchsia pink that tumbled and fluttered from the open mouths of a pair of yellow lilies.

She hardly hesitated before taking it off its hanger and putting it on. It was glorious. She remembered that this was the word she had thought of the first time she had seen it. How she had longed to possess it and how she had not dared look for long lest the yearning became painful and ridiculous! With her head a little on one side, she stood over Patrick, wondering whether to kiss him goodbye. Perhaps not, perhaps it would be better not. After all, he would hardly notice.

She let herself out of the flat. They would not meet again. A more than fair exchange had been silently negotiated by her. Feeling happy, feeling very light of heart, she ran down the stairs and out into the morning, insulated from the cold by her coat of many colours, her butterflies, her rightful possession.

A Wife in a Million

Val McDermid

The woman strolled through the supermarket, choosing a few
items for her basket. As she reached the display of sauces and
pickles, a muscle in her jaw tightened. She looked round, willing
herself to appear casual. No one watched. Swiftly she took a jar
of tomato pickle from her large leather handbag and placed it on
the shelf. She moved on to the frozen meat section.

A few minutes later, she passed down the same aisle and
paused. She repeated the exercise, this time adding two more
jars to the shelf. As she walked on to the checkout, she felt
tension slide from her body, leaving her light-headed.

She stood in the queue, anonymous among the morning's
shoppers, another neat woman in a well-cut winter coat, a faint
smile on her face, and a strangely unfocused look in her pale
blue eyes.

Sarah Graham was sprawled on the sofa reading the Situations
Vacant in the *Burnalder Evening News* when she heard the car
pull up in the drive. Sighing, she dropped the paper and went
through to the kitchen. By the time she had pulled the cork from
a bottle of elderflower wine and poured two glasses the front
door had opened and closed. Sarah stood, glasses in hand,
facing the kitchen door.

Detective Sergeant Maggie Staniforth came into the kitchen,
took the proffered glass and kissed Sarah perfunctorily. She
walked into the living room and slumped in a chair, calling over
her shoulder, 'And what kind of a day have you had?'

Sarah followed her through and shrugged. 'Another day in
paradise. You don't want to hear my catalogue of boredom.'

'It doesn't bore me. It reminds me that there's life outside
crime.'

'I got up about nine, by which time you'd no doubt arrested
half a dozen villains. I whizzed through the *Guardian* job ads,

and went down the library to check out the other papers. After lunch I cleaned the bedroom, did a bit of ironing and polished the dining-room table. Then down to the newsagents for the evening paper. A thrill a minute. And you? Solved the crime of the century?'

Maggie winced. 'Nothing so exciting. Bit of breaking and entering, bit of paperwork on the rape case at the blues club. It's due in court next week.'

'At least you get paid for it.'

'Something will come up soon, love.'

'And meanwhile I go on being your kept woman.'

Maggie said nothing. There was nothing to say. The two of them had been together since they fell head over heels in love at university eleven years before. Things had been fine while they were both concentrating on climbing their career ladders. But Sarah's career in personnel management had hit a brick wall when the company which employed her had collapsed nine months previously. That crisis had opened a wound in their relationship that was rapidly festering. Now Maggie was often afraid to speak for fear of provoking another bitter exchange. She drank her wine in silence.

'No titbits to amuse me, then?' Sarah demanded. 'No funny little tales from the underbelly?'

'One thing that might interest you,' Maggie said tentatively. 'Notice a story in the *News* last night about a woman taken to the General with suspected food poisoning?'

'I saw it. I read every inch of that paper. It fills an hour.'

'She's just died. And there have been two other families affected. The funny thing is they can't track down a common source. Jim Bryant from casualty was telling me about it.'

Sarah pulled a face. 'Sure you can face my spaghetti carbonara tonight?'

The telephone cut across Maggie's smile. She quickly crossed the room and picked it up on the third ring. 'D S Staniforth speaking . . . Hi, Bill.' She listened intently. 'Good God!' she breathed. 'I'll be with you in ten minutes. Okay.' She stood holding the phone. 'Sarah, that woman I told you about. It wasn't food poisoning. It was a massive dose of arsenic, and two of the other so-called food poisoning cases have died. They suspect arsenic there too. I'm meeting Bill at the hospital.'

'You'd better move, then. Shall I save you some food?'

'No point. And don't wait up, I'll be late.' Maggie crossed to her and gave her a brief hug. She hurried out of the room. Seconds later, the front door slammed.

The fluorescent strips made the kitchen look bright but cold. The woman opened one of the fitted cupboards and took a jar of greyish-white powder from the very back of the shelf.

She picked up a filleting knife whose edge was honed to a wicked sharpness. She slid it delicately under the flap of a cardboard pack of blancmange powder. She did the same to five other packets. Then she carefully opened the inner paper envelopes. Into each she mixed a tablespoonful of the powder from the jar.

Under the light, the grey strands in her auburn hair glinted. Painstakingly, she folded the inner packets closed again and with a drop of glue she resealed the cardboard packages. She put them all in a shopping bag and carried it into the rear porch.

She replaced the jar in the cupboard and went through to the living room where the television blared. She looked strangely triumphant.

It was after three when Maggie Staniforth closed the front door behind her. As she hung up her sheepskin, she noticed lines of strain round her eyes in the hall mirror. Sarah appeared in the kitchen doorway. 'I know you're probably too tired to feel hungry, but I've made some soup if you want it,' she said.

'You shouldn't have stayed up. It's late.'

'I've got nothing else to do. After all, there's plenty of opportunity for me to catch up on my sleep.'

Please God, not now, thought Maggie. As if the job isn't hard enough without coming home to hassles from Sarah.

But she was proved wrong. Sarah smiled and said, 'Do you want some grub?'

'That depends.'

'On what?'

'Whether there's Higham's Continental Tomato Pickle in it.'

Sarah looked bewildered. Maggie went on, 'It seems that three people have died from arsenic administered in Higham's Continental Tomato Pickle bought from Fastfare Supermarket.'

'You're joking!'

'Wish I was.' Maggie went through to the kitchen. She poured herself a glass of orange juice as Sarah served up a steaming bowl of lentil soup with a pile of buttered brown bread. Maggie sat down and tucked in, giving her lover a disjointed summary as she ate.

'Victim number one: May Scott, fifty-seven, widow, lived up Warburton Road. Numbers two and three: Gary Andrews, fifteen, and his brother Kevin, thirteen, from Priory Farm Estate. Their father is seriously ill. So are two others now, Thomas and Louise Forrester of Bryony Grange. No connection between them except that they all ate pickle from jars bought on the same day at Fastfare.

'Could be someone playing at extortion – you know, pay me a million pounds or I'll do it again. Could be someone with a grudge against Fastfare. Ditto against Higham's. So you can bet your sweet life we're going to be hammered into the ground on this one. Already we're getting flak.'

Maggie finished her meal. Her head dropped into her hands.

'What a bitch of a job.'

'Better than no job at all.'

'Is it?'

'You should know better than to ask.'

Maggie sighed. 'Take me to bed, Sarah. Let me forget about the battlefield for a few hours, eh?'

Piped music lulled the shoppers at Pinkertons Hypermarket into a drugged acquisitiveness. The woman pushing the trolley was deaf to its bland presence. When she reached the shelf with the blancmange display, she stopped and checked that the coast was clear.

She swiftly put three packs on the shelf and moved away. A few minutes later she returned and studied several instant cake mixes as she waited for the aisle to clear. Then she completed her mission and finished her shopping in a leisurely fashion.

At the checkout, she brightly chatted to the bored teenager who rang up her purchases automatically. Then she left, gently humming the song that flowed from the shop's speakers.

Three days later, Maggie Staniforth burst into her living room in the middle of the afternoon to find Sarah typing a job application. 'Red alert, love,' she announced. 'I'm only home to have a quick bath and change my things. Any chance of a sandwich?'

'I was beginning to wonder if you still lived here,' Sarah muttered darkly. 'If you were having an affair, at least I'd know how to fight back.'

'Not now, love, please.'

'Do you want something hot? Soup? Omelette?'

'Soup, please. And a toasted cheese sandwich.'

'Coming up. What's the panic this time?'

Maggie's eyes clouded. 'Our homicidal maniac has struck again. Eight people on the critical list at the General. This time arsenic was in Garratt's Blancmange from Pinkertons Hypermarket. Bill's doing a television appeal right now asking for people to bring in any packets bought there this week.'

'Different manufacturer, different supermarket. Sounds like a crazy rather than a grudge, doesn't it?'

'And that makes it impossible to predict. Anyway, I'm going for that bath now. I'll be down in fifteen minutes.' Maggie stopped in the kitchen doorway. 'I'm not being funny, Sarah, don't do any shopping in the supermarkets. Butchers, greengrocers, okay. But no self-service, prepackaged food. Please.'

Sarah nodded. She had never seen Maggie afraid in eight years in the force and the sight did nothing to lift her depressed spirits.

This time it was jars of mincemeat. Even the Salvation Army band playing carols outside Nationwide Stores failed to make the woman pause in her mission. Her shopping bag held six jars laced with deadly white powder when she entered the super-market.

When she left, there were none. She dropped 50p in the collecting tin as she passed the band because they were playing her favourite carol, 'In the Bleak Midwinter'. She walked slowly back to the car park, not pausing to look at the shop-window Christmas displays. She wasn't anticipating a merry Christmas.

Sarah walked back from the newsagent's with the evening paper, reading the front page as she went. The Burnalder Poisoner was front page news everywhere by now, but the stories in the local paper seemed to carry an extra edge of fear. They were thorough in their coverage, tracing any possible commercial connection between the three giant food companies that produced the contaminated food. They also speculated on the possible reasons for the week-long gaps between outbreaks. And they laid out in stark detail the drastic effect the poisoning was having on the finances of the food processing companies.

The latest killer was Univex mincemeat. Sarah shivered as she read of the latest three deaths, bringing the toll to twelve. As she turned the corner, she saw Maggie's car in the drive and increased her pace. A grim idea had taken root in her brain as she read the long report.

While she was hanging up her jacket, Maggie called from the kitchen. Sarah walked slowly through to find her tucking into a plate of eggs and bacon, but without her usual dollop of tomato ketchup. There were dark circles beneath her eyes and the skin around them was grey and stretched. She had not slept at home for two nights. The job had never made such demands on her before. Sarah found a moment to wonder if the atmosphere between them was partly responsible for Maggie's total commit-ment to this desperate search.

'How is it going?' she asked anxiously.

'It's not,' said Maggie. 'Virtually nothing to go on. No link that we can find. It's not as if we even have leads to chase up. I came home for a break because we were just sitting staring at each other, wondering what to do next. Short of searching everyone who goes into supermarkets, what can we do? And those bloody reporters seem to have taken up residence in the station. We're being leaned on from all directions. We've got to crack this one or we'll be crucified.'

Sarah sat down. 'I've been thinking about this. The grudge theory has broken down because you can't find a link between the companies, am I right?'

'Yes.'

'Have you thought about the effect unemployment has on crime?'

'Burglary, shoplifting, mugging, vandalism, yes. But surely not mass poisoning, love.'

'There's so much bitterness there, Maggie. So much hatred. I've often felt like murdering those incompetent tossers who destroyed Liddell's and threw me on the scrap-heap. Did you think about people who'd been given the boot?'

'We did think about it. But only a handful of people have ever worked for all three companies. None of them have any reason to hold a grudge. And none of them have any connection with Burnalder.'

'There's another aspect though, Maggie. It only hit me when I read the paper tonight. The *News* has a big piece about the parent companies who make the three products. Now, I'd swear that each one of those companies has advertised in the last couple of months for management executives. I know, I applied for two of the jobs. I didn't even get interviewed because I've got no experience in the food industry, only in plastics. There must be other people in the same boat, maybe less stable than I am.'

'My God!' Maggie breathed. She pushed her plate away. The colour had returned to her cheeks and she seemed to have found fresh energy. She got up and hugged Sarah fiercely. 'You've given us the first positive lead in this whole bloody case. You're a genius!'

'I hope you'll remember that when they give you your inspector's job.'

Maggie grinned on her way out the door. 'I owe you one. I'll see you later.'

As the front door slammed, Sarah said ironically, 'I hope it's not too late already, babe.'

Detective Inspector Bill Nicholson had worked with Maggie Staniforth for two years. His initial distrust of her gender had been broken down by her sheer grasp of the job. Now he was wont to describe her as 'a bloody good copper in spite of being a woman' as if this were a discovery uniquely his, and a direct product of working for him. As she unfolded Sarah's hunch, backed by photostats of newspaper advertisements culled from the local paper's files, he realized for the first time she was probably going to leapfrog him on the career ladder before too long. He didn't like the idea, but he wasn't prepared to let that stand between him and a job of work.

They started on the long haul of speaking directly to the personnel officers of the three companies. It meant quartering the country and they knew they were working against the clock. Back at Burnalder, a team of detectives was phoning companies who had advertised similar vacancies, asking for lists of applicants. The lumbering machinery of the law was in gear.

On the evening of the second day, an exhausted Maggie arrived home. Six hundred and thirty-seven miles of driving had taken their toll and she looked ten years older. Sarah helped her out of her coat and poured her a stiff drink in silence.

'You were right,' Maggie sighed. 'We've got the name and address of a man who has been rejected by all three after the first interview. We're moving in on him tonight. If he sticks to his pattern, he'll be aiming to strike again tomorrow. So with luck, it'll be a red-handed job.' She sounded grim and distant. 'What a bloody waste. Twelve lives because he can't get a bloody job.'

'I can understand it,' Sarah said abruptly, and went through to the kitchen.

Maggie stared after her, shocked but comprehending. She felt again the low rumble of anger deep inside her against a system that set her to catch people it had so often made its victims. If only Sarah had not lost her well-paid job then Maggie knew she would have left the force by now, but they needed her salary to keep their heads above water. The job itself was dirty enough; but the added pain of keeping her relationship with Sarah constantly under wraps was finally becoming more than she could comfortably bear. Sarah wasn't the only one whose choices had been drastically pruned by her unemployment.

By nine fifty-five a dozen detectives were stationed around a neat detached house in a quiet suburban street. In the garden a For Sale sign sprouted among the rose bushes. Lights burned in the kitchen and living room.

In the car, Bill made a final check to his search warrant. Then, after a last word over the walkie-talkie, he and Maggie walked up the drive. 'It's up to you now,' he said, and rang the doorbell. It was answered by a tall, bluff man in his mid forties. There were lines of strain round his eyes and his clothes hung loosely, as if he had recently lost weight.

'Yes?' he asked in a pleasant, gentle voice.

'Mr Derek Millfield?' Maggie demanded.

'That's me. How can I help you?'

'We are police officers, Mr Millfield. We'd like to have a word with you, if you don't mind.'

He looked puzzled. 'By all means. But I don't see what . . .' His voice tailed off. 'You'd better come in, I suppose.'

They entered the house and Millfield showed them into a surprisingly large living room. It was tastefully and expensively furnished. A woman sat watching the television.

'My wife Shula,' he explained. 'Shula, these are policemen – I mean officers, sorry, miss.'

Shula Millfield stood up and faced them. 'You've come for me then,' she said.

It was hard to say who looked most surprised. Then suddenly she was laughing, crying and screaming, all at once.

Maggie stretched out on the sofa. 'It was horrific. She must have been living on a knife edge for weeks before she finally flipped. He's been out of work for seven months. They've had to take their kids out of public school, had to sell a car, sell their possessions. He obviously had no idea what she was up to. I can't believe anyone would just go berserk like that. All for the sake of a nice middle-class lifestyle.

'There's no doubt about it, by the way. Her fingerprints are all over the jar of arsenic. She stole the jar a month ago. She worked part-time in the pharmacy at the cottage hospital in Kingcaple. They didn't notice the loss, God knows how.'

'What will happen to her?' Sarah asked coolly.

'She'll be tried, if she's fit to plead. But I doubt if she will be. I'm afraid it will be the locked ward for life.' When she looked up, Maggie saw there were tears on Sarah's cheeks. She immediately got up and put her arm around her. 'Hey, don't cry, love. Please.'

'I can't help it, Maggie. You see, I know how she feels. I know that utter lack of all hope. I know the hatred, that sense of frustration and futility. There's nothing you can do to take that away.

'What you have to live with, Detective Sergeant Staniforth, is that it could have been me. It could so easily have been me.'

The Necklace of Pearls

Dorothy L. Sayers

Sir Septimus Shale was accustomed to assert his authority once
in the year and once only. He allowed his young and fashionable
wife to fill his house with diagrammatic furniture made of steel;
to collect advanced artists and anti-grammatical poets; to believe
in cocktails and relativity and to dress as extravagantly as she
pleased; but he did insist on an old-fashioned Christmas. He
was a simple-hearted man, who really liked plum-pudding and
cracker mottoes, and he could not get it out of his head that
other people, 'at bottom,' enjoyed these things also. At
Christmas, therefore, he firmly retired to his country house in
Essex, called in the servants to hang the holly and mistletoe upon
the cubist electric fittings; loaded the steel sideboard with
delicacies from Fortnum & Mason; hung up stockings at the
heads of the polished walnut bedsteads; and even, on this
occasion only, had the electric radiators removed from the
modernist grates and installed wood fires and a Yule log. He
then gathered his family and friends about him, filled them with
as much Dickensian good fare as he could persuade them to
swallow, and after their Christmas dinner, set them down to play
'Charades' and 'Clumps' and 'Animal, Vegetable and Mineral'
in the drawing-room, concluding these diversions by 'Hide-and-
Seek' in the dark all over the house. Because Sir Septimus was a
very rich man, his guests fell in with this invariable programme,
and if they were bored, they did not tell him so.

Another charming and traditional custom which he followed
was that of presenting to his daughter Margharita a pearl on each
successive birthday – this anniversary happening to coincide
with Christmas Eve. The pearls now numbered twenty, and the
collection was beginning to enjoy a certain celebrity, and had been
photographed in the Society papers. Though not sensationally
large – each one being about the size of a marrowfat pea – the
pearls were of very great value. They were of exquisite colour

and perfect shape and matched to a hair's-weight. On this particular Christmas Eve, the presentation of the twenty-first pearl had been the occasion of a very special ceremony. There was a dance and there were speeches. On the Christmas night following, the more restricted family party took place, with the turkey and the Victorian games. There were eleven guests, in addition to Sir Septimus and Lady Shale and their daughter, nearly all related or connected to them in some way: John Shale, a brother, with his wife and their son and daughter Henry and Betty; Betty's *fiancé*, Oswald Truegood, a young man with parliamentary ambitions; George Comphrey, a cousin of Lady Shale's, aged about thirty and known as a man about town; Lavinia Prescott, asked on George's accout; Joyce Trivett, asked on Henry Shale's account; Richard and Beryl Dennison, distant relations of Lady Shale, who lived a gay and expensive life in town on nobody precisely knew what resources; and Lord Peter Wimsey, asked, in a touching spirit of unreasonable hope, on Margharita's account. There were also, of course, William Norgate, secretary to Sir Septimus, and Miss Tomkins, secretary to Lady Shale, who had to be there because, without their calm efficiency, the Christmas arrangements could not have been carried through.

Dinner was over – a seemingly endless succession of soup, fish, turkey, roast beef, plum-pudding, mince-pies, crystallized fruit, nuts and five kinds of wine, presided over by Sir Septimus, all smiles, by Lady Shale, all mocking deprecation, and by Margharita, pretty and bored, with the necklace of twenty-one pearls gleaming softly on her slender throat. Gorged and dyspeptic and longing only for the horizontal position, the company had been shepherded into the drawing-room and set to play 'Musical Chairs' (Miss Tomkins at the piano), 'Hunt the Slipper' (slipper provided by Miss Tomkins), and 'Dumb Crambo' (costumes by Miss Tomkins and Mr William Norgate). The back drawing-room (for Sir Septimus clung to these old-fashioned names) provided an admirable dressing-room, being screened by folding doors from the large drawing-room in which the audience sat on aluminium chairs, scrabbling uneasy toes on a floor of black glass under the tremendous illumination of electricity reflected from a brass ceiling.

It was William Norgate who, after taking the temperature of the meeting, suggested to Lady Shale that they should play something less athletic. Lady Shale agreed and, as usual, suggested bridge. Sir Septimus, as usual, blew the suggestion aside.

'Bridge? Nonsense! Nonsense! Play bridge every day of your lives. This is Christmas time. Something we can all play together. How about "Animal, Vegetable and Mineral"?'

This intellectual pastime was a favourite of Sir Septimus; he was rather good at putting pregnant questions. After a brief discussion, it became evident that this game was an inevitable part of the programme. The party settled down to it, Sir Septimus undertaking to 'go out' first and set the thing going.

Presently they had guessed among other things Miss Tomkins's mother's photograph, a gramophone record of 'I want to be happy' (much scientific research into the exact composition of records, settled by William Norgate out of the *Encyclopaedia Britannica*), the smallest stickleback in the stream at the bottom of the garden, the new planet Pluto, the scarf worn by Mrs Dennison (very confusing, because it was not silk, which would be animal, or artificial silk, which would be vegetable, but made of spun glass – mineral, a very clever choice of subject), and had failed to guess the Prime Minister's wireless speech – which was voted not fair, since nobody could decide whether it was animal by nature or a kind of gas. It was decided that they should do one more word and then go on to 'Hide-and-Seek.' Oswald Truegood had retired into the back room and shut the door behind him while the party discussed the next subject of examination, when suddenly Sir Septimus broke in on the argument by calling to his daughter:

'Hullo, Margy! What have you done with your necklace?'

'I took it off, Dad, because I thought it might get broken in "Dumb Crambo." It's over here on this table. No, it isn't. Did you take it, mother?'

'No, I didn't. If I'd seen it, I should have. You are a careless child.'

'I believe you've got it yourself, Dad. You're teasing.'

Sir Septimus denied the accusation with some energy. Everybody got up and began to hunt about. There were not many places in that bare and polished room where a necklace could be hidden. After ten minutes' fruitless investigation, Richard Dennison, who had been seated next to the table where the pearls had been placed, began to look rather uncomfortable.

'Awkward, you know,' he remarked to Wimsey.

At this moment, Oswald Truegood put his head through the folding-doors and asked whether they hadn't settled on something by now, because he was getting the fidgets.

This directed the attention of the searchers to the inner room. Margharita must have been mistaken. She had taken it in there, and it had got mixed up with the dressing-up clothes somehow. The room was ransacked. Everything was lifted up and shaken. The thing began to look serious. After half an hour of desperate energy it became apparent that the pearls were nowhere to be found.

'They must be somewhere in these two rooms, you know,' said Wimsey. 'The back drawing-room has no door and nobody could have gone out of the front drawing-room without being seen. Unless the windows—'

No. The windows were all guarded on the outside by heavy shutters which it needed two footmen to take down and replace. The pearls had not gone out that way. In fact, the mere suggestion that they had left the drawing-room at all was disagreeable. Because – because—

It was William Norgate, efficient as ever, who coldly and boldly faced the issue.

'I think, Sir Septimus, it would be a relief to the minds of everybody present if we could all be searched.'

Sir Septimus was horrified, but the guests, having found a leader, backed up Norgate. The door was locked, and the search conducted – the ladies in the inner room and the men in the outer.

Nothing resulted from it except some very interesting information about the belongings habitually carried about by the average man and woman. It was natural that Lord Peter Wimsey should possess a pair of forceps, a pocket lens and a small folding footrule – was he not a Sherlock Holmes in high life? But that Oswald Truegood should have two liver-pills in a screw of paper and Henry Shale a pocket edition of *The Odes of Horace* was unexpected. Why did John Shale distend the pockets of his dress-suit with a stump of red sealing-wax, an ugly little mascot and a five-shilling piece? George Comphrey had a pair of folding scissors, and three wrapped lumps of sugar, of the sort served in restaurants and dining-cars – evidence of a not uncommon form of kleptomania; but that the tidy and exact Norgate should burden himself with a reel of white cotton, three separate lengths of string and twelve safety-pins on a card seemed remarkable till one remembered that he had superintended all the Christmas decorations. Richard Dennison, amid some confusion and laughter, was found to cherish a lady's garter, a powder compact and half a potato; the last-named, he said, was a prophylactic against rheumatism (to which he was subject), while the other objects belonged to his wife. On the ladies side, the more striking exhibits were a little book on palmistry, three invisible hair-pins and a baby's photograph (Miss Tomkins); a Chinese trick cigarette-case with a secret compartment (Beryl Dennison); a *very* private letter and an outfit for mending stocking-ladders (Lavinia Prescott); and a pair of eyebrow tweezers and a small packet of white powder, said to be for headaches (Betty Shale). An agitating moment followed the production from Joyce Trivett's handbag of a small string of pearls – but it was promptly remembered that these had come out of one of the crackers at dinner-time, and they were, in fact, synthetic. In short, the search was unproductive of anything beyond a general shamefacedness and the discomfort always produced by undressing and re-dressing in a hurry at the wrong time of the day.

It was then that somebody, very grudgingly and haltingly, mentioned the horrid word 'Police.' Sir Septimus, naturally, was appalled by the idea. It was disgusting. He would not allow it. The pearls must be somewhere. They must search the rooms again. Could not Lord Peter Wimsey, with his experience of – er – mysterious happenings, do something to assist them?

'Eh?' said his lordship. 'Oh, by Jove, yes – by all means, certainly. That is to say, provided nobody supposes – eh, what? I mean to say, you don't know that I'm not a suspicious character, do you, what?'

Lady Shale interposed with authority.

'We don't think *anybody* ought to be suspected,' she said, 'but, if we did, we'd know it couldn't be you. You know *far* too much about crimes to want to commit one.'

'All right,' said Wimsey. 'But after the way the place has been gone over—' He shrugged his shoulders.

'Yes, I'm afraid you won't be able to find any footprints,' said Margharita. 'But we may have overlooked something.'

Wimsey nodded.

'I'll try. Do you all mind sitting down on your chairs in the outer room and staying there. All except one of you – I'd better have a witness to anything I do or find. Sir Septimus – you'd be the best person, I think.'

He shepherded them to their places and began a slow circuit of the two rooms, exploring every surface, gazing up to the polished brazen ceiling and crawling on hands and knees in the approved fashion across the black and shining desert of the floors. Sir Septimus followed, staring when Wimsey crawled, bending with his hands upon his knees when Wimsey stared, and puffing at intervals with astonishment and chagrin. Their progress rather resembled that of a man taking out a very inquisitive puppy for a very leisurely constitutional. Fortunately, Lady Shale's taste in furnishing made investigation easier; there were scarcely any nooks or corners where anything could be concealed.

They reached the inner drawing-room, and here the dressing-up clothes were again minutely examined, but without result. Finally, Wimsey lay down flat on his stomach to squint under a steel cabinet which was one of the very few pieces of furniture which possessed short legs. Something about it seemed to catch his attention. He rolled up his sleeve and plunged his arm into the cavity, kicked convulsively in the effort to reach farther than was humanly possible, pulled out from his pocket and extended his folding foot-rule, fished with it under the cabinet and eventually succeeded in extracting what he sought.

It was a very minute object – in fact, a pin. Not an ordinary pin, but one resembling those used by entomologists to impale extremely small moths on the setting-board. It was about three-quarters of an inch in length, as fine as a very fine needle, with a sharp point and a particularly small head.

'Bless my soul!' said Sir Septimus. 'What's that?'

'Does anybody here happen to collect moths or beetles or anything?' asked Wimsey, squatting on his haunches and examining the pin.

'I'm pretty sure they don't,' replied Sir Septimus. 'I'll ask them.'

'Don't do that.' Wimsey bent his head and stared at the floor, from which his own face stared meditatively back at him.

'I see,' said Wimsey presently. 'That's how it was done. All right, Sir Septimus. I know where the pearls are but I don't know who took them. Perhaps it would be as well – for everybody's satisfaction – just to find out. In the meantime they are perfectly safe. Don't tell anyone that we've found this pin or that we've discovered anything. Send all these people to bed. Lock the drawing-room door and keep the key, and we'll get our man – or woman – by breakfast-time.'

'God bless my soul,' said Sir Septimus, very much puzzled.

Lord Peter Wimsey kept careful watch that night upon the drawing-room door. Nobody, however, came near it. Either the thief suspected a trap or he felt confident that any time would do to recover the pearls. Wimsey, however, did not feel that he was wasting his time. He was making a list of people who had been left alone in the back drawing-room during the playing of 'Animal, Vegetable or Mineral.' The list ran as follows.

Sir Septimus Shale
Lavinia Prescott

William Norgate
Joyce Trivett and Henry Shale (together, because they had
    claimed to be incapable of guessing anything unaided)
Mrs Dennison
Betty Shale
George Comphrey
Richard Dennison
Miss Tomkins
Oswald Truegood

He also made out a list of the persons to whom the pearls
might be useful or desirable. Unfortunately, this list agreed in
almost all respects with the first (always excepting Sir Septimus)
and so was not very helpful. The two secretaries had both come
well recommended, but that was exactly what they would have
done had they come with ulterior designs; the Dennisons were
notorious livers from hand to mouth; Betty Shale carried
mysterious white powders in her handbag, and was known to be
in with a rather rapid set in town; Henry was a harmless
dilettante, but Joyce Trivett could twist him round her little
finger and was what Jane Austen liked to call 'expensive and
dissipated'; Comphrey speculated; Oswald Truegood was rather
frequently present at Epsom and Newmarket – the search for
motives was only too fatally easy.

When the second housemaid and the under-footman appeared in the passage with household implements, Wimsey
abandoned his vigil, but he was down early to breakfast. Sir
Septimus with his wife and daughter were down before him, and
a certain air of tension made itself felt. Wimsey, standing on the
hearth before the fire, made conversation about the weather and
politics.

The party assembled gradually, but, as though by common
consent, nothing was said about the pearls until after breakfast,
when Oswald Truegood took the bull by the horns.

'Well now!' said he. 'How's the detective getting along? Got
your man, Wimsey?'

'Not yet,' said Wimsey easily.

Sir Septimus, looking at Wimsey as though for his cue,
cleared his throat and dashed into speech.

'All very tiresome,' he said, 'all very unpleasant. Hr'rm.
Nothing for it but the police, I'm afraid. Just at Christmas, too.
Hr'rm. Spoilt the party. Can't stand seeing all this stuff about
the place.' He waved his hand towards the festoons of
evergreens and coloured paper that adorned the walls. 'Take it
all down, eh, what? No heart in it. Hr'rm. Burn the lot.'

'What a pity, when we worked so hard over it,' said Joyce.

'Oh, leave it, Uncle,' said Henry Shale. 'You're bothering too
much about the pearls. They're sure to turn up.'

'Shall I ring for James?' suggested William Norgate.

'No,' interrupted Comphrey, 'let's do it ourselves. It'll give us
something to do and take our minds off our troubles.'

'That's right,' said Sir Septimus. 'Start right away. Hate the
sight of it.'

He savagely hauled a great branch of holly down from the
mantelpiece and flung it, crackling, into the fire.

'That's the stuff,' said Richard Dennison. 'Make a good old
blaze!' He leapt up from the table and snatched the mistletoe
from the chandelier. 'Here goes! One more kiss for somebody
before it's too late.'

'Isn't it unlucky to take it down before the New Year?'
suggested Miss Tomkins.

'Unlucky be hanged. We'll have it all down. Off the stairs and
out of the drawing-room too. Somebody go and collect it.'

'Isn't the drawing-room locked?' asked Oswald.

'No, Lord Peter says the pearls aren't there, wherever else
they are, so it's unlocked. That's right, isn't it, Wimsey?'

'Quite right. The pearls were taken out of these rooms. I can't
tell you how, but I'm positive of it. In fact, I'll pledge my
reputation that wherever they are, they're not up there.'

'Oh, well,' said Comphrey, 'in that case, have at it! Come
along, Lavinia – you and Dennison do the drawing-room and I'll
do the back room. We'll have a race.'

'But if the police are coming in,' said Dennison, 'oughtn't
everything to be left just as it is?'

'Damn the police!' shouted Sir Septimus. 'They don't want evergreens.'

Oswald and Margharita were already pulling the holly and ivy from the staircase, amid peals of laughter. The party dispersed. Wimsey went quietly upstairs and into the drawing-room, where the work of demolition was taking place at a great rate, George having bet the other two ten shillings to a tanner that they would not finish their part of the job before he finished his.

'You mustn't help,' said Lavinia, laughing to Wimsey. 'It wouldn't be fair.'

Wimsey said nothing, but waited until the room was clear. Then he followed them down again to the hall, where the fire was sending up a great roaring and spluttering, suggestive of Guy Fawkes night. He whispered to Sir Septimus, who went forward and touched George Comphrey on the shoulder.

'Lord Peter wants to say something to you, my boy,' he said.

Comphrey started and went with him a little reluctantly, as it seemed. He was not looking very well.

'Mr Comphrey,' said Wimsey, 'I fancy these are some of your property.' He held out the palm of his hand, in which rested twenty-two fine, small-headed pins.

'Ingenious,' said Wimsey, 'but something less ingenious would have served his turn better. It was very unlucky, Sir Septimus, that you should have mentioned the pearls when you did. Of course, he hoped that the loss wouldn't be discovered till we'd chucked guessing games and taken to "Hide-and-Seek". Then the pearls might have been anywhere in the house, we shouldn't have locked the drawing-room door, and he could have recovered them at his leisure. He had had this possibility in his mind when he came here, obviously, and that was why he brought his pins, and Miss Shale's taking off the necklace to play "Dumb Crambo" gave him his opportunity.

'He had spent Christmas here before, and knew perfectly well that "Animal, Vegetable and Mineral" would form part of the entertainment. He had only to gather up the necklace from the table when it came to his turn to retire, and he knew he could count on at least five minutes by himself while we were all arguing about the choice of a word. He had only to snip the pearls from the string with his pocket-scissors, burn the string in the grate and fasten the pearls to the mistletoe with the fine pins. The mistletoe was hung on the chandelier, pretty high – it's a lofty room – but he could easily reach it by standing on the glass table, which wouldn't show footmarks, and it was almost certain that nobody would think of examining the mistletoe for extra berries. I shouldn't have thought of it myself if I hadn't found the pin which he had dropped. That gave me the idea that the pearls had been separated and the rest was easy. I took the pearls off the mistletoe last night – the clasp was there, too, pinned among the holly-leaves. Here they are. Comphrey must have got a nasty shock this morning. I knew he was our man when he suggested that the guests should tackle the decorations them- selves and that he should do the back drawing-room – but I wish I had seen his face when he came to the mistletoe and found the pearls gone.'

'And you worked it all out when you found the pin?' said Sir Septimus.

'Yes; I knew then where the pearls had gone to.'

'But you never even looked at the mistletoe.'

'I saw it reflected in the black glass floor, and it struck me then how much the mistletoe berries looked like pearls.'

Activities

The Reluctant Detective

Background notes

Michael Z. Lewin was born in Massachussetts in 1942. He attended Harvard University and also studied at Churchill College, Cambridge. Michael Lewin worked as a science teacher in Connecticut and New York before moving to England in 1971. He makes his home in the small West Country town which is the setting for his story *The Reluctant Detective* and writes sport reports for newspapers as well as crime fiction.

Pair work

Most detective stories invite us to solve a mystery. See how sharp you are at picking up clues. There are three points in the story at which to stop; at each one make notes with your partner and predict what will happen.
1 When the reluctant detective says 'What the hell do we do now?' jot down your views about the crime so far; what are your suspicions at that moment? (page 6).
2 The next stopping point is 'Dawn was cooking something up, and it wasn't chips.' (page 12). Have your suspicions changed? What new information do you have about the various characters?
3 Your final chance to solve the case comes when Dawn says 'See how reasonable we are?' (page 14). Who is guilty and of what crime? Have Frederick and Dawn become criminals themselves?

Group work

Once you have read the story consider these points:

☐ Do you think the writer was trying to write chiefly a comic story or a detective story? Discuss this together and decide whether you feel Michael Lewin managed to keep your interest in the way that a writer of a 'serious' detective story would. Are there any moments which you all found funny? Once you have thought about the story in this way try to jot down a paragraph that sums up the combination of humour and detection and gives a clear idea of what the group felt about it.

☐ Who is the detective in this story? Frederick tells us the story and we know that he is 'reluctant'; is Dawn reluctant too? Your job is to assess these two as individuals and as a team. Look at the story together and make some notes about Dawn and about Frederick; is one of them the *real* detective or are they a true team? Prepare your notes and present your verdict to the class.

Written assignments

1 '. . . So, we decided, maybe one more. Or two.' (page 15). Frederick and Dawn solved this case quite easily with the help of Dawn's family. Will they succeed with the next one? Write the story of their next case.

2 'Scoop Wall tracked down Dawn and me too.' (page 15). Write the story about the case which appeared in the Frome newspaper. Bear in mind that the report would be in a small, local paper; what kind of detail would interest its readers?

3 Detective series are very popular on television for many reasons. This story is rather unusual in its mixture of comedy and detection. Imagine that you are a scriptwriter who wants to sell a series based on the story to a television production company.

Your completed assignment might contain - a letter from you (as the script writer), a summary of the story with your comments and a page or two of sample script.

In your letter you will have to persuade the company that Dawn and Frederick will make interesting enough characters for a whole series. By including a summary of the story and a commentary on it, you can point out what makes the story different and special. You might compare and contrast it to current, popular series. The company will also want a sample page of script as this will show them how the story would be entertaining on the screen. You might find it useful to look at any examples of TV scripts that your teacher can give you.

The following extract comes from a short story by Raymond Chandler, perhaps the most famous American Crime writer of this century, best known for his creation of the detective, Philip Marlowe. This hard-bitten private eye portrayed in many American films by Humphrey Bogart, Dick Powell and others, is thought of by many as the definitive wise-cracking investigator. What makes Chandler's writing so special is that whilst stories deal with serious subjects they are written with a light touch and are full of irony and humour. This extract, the opening of his short story, *The Lady in the Lake*, gives some flavour of Chandler's style and shows where authors like Michael Z. Lewin find their inspiration.

I was breaking a new pair of shoes in on my desk that morning when Violets M'Gee called me up. It was a dull, hot, damp August day and you couldn't keep your neck dry with a bath-towel.

'How's the boy?' Violets began, as usual. 'No business in a week, huh? There's a guy named Howard Melton over in the Avenant Building lost track of his wife. He's district manager for the Doreme Cosmetic Company. He don't want to give it to Missing Persons for some reason. The boss knows him a little. Better get over there, and take your shoes off before you go in. It's a pretty snooty outfit.'

Violets M'Gee is a homicide dick in the sheriff's office, and if it wasn't for all the charity jobs he gives me, I might be able to make a living. This looked a little different, so I put my feet on the floor and swabbed the back of my neck again and went over there.

The Avenant Building is on Olive near Sixth and has a black-and-white rubber sidewalk out in front. The elevator girls wear grey silk Russian blouses and the kind of flop-over berets artists used to wear to keep the paint out of their hair. The Doreme Cosmetic Company was on the seventh floor and had a good piece of it. There was a big glass-walled reception room with flowers and Persian rugs and bits of nutty sculpture in glazed ware. A neat little blonde sat in a built-in switchboard off in the corner, out of harm's way. They had a receptionist at a big desk with flowers on it and a tilted sign reading: MISS VAN DE GRAAF. She wore Harold Lloyd cheaters and her hair was dragged back to where her forehead looked high enough to have snow on it.

She said Mr Howard Melton was in conference, but she would take my card in to him when she had an opportunity, and what was my business, please? I said I didn't have a card, but the name was John Dalmas, from Mr West.

'Who is Mr West?' she inquired coldly. 'Does Mr Melton know him?'

'That's past me, sister. Not knowing Mr Melton I would not know his friends.'

'What is the nature of your business?'

'Personal.'

'I see.' She initialled three papers on her desk quickly, to keep from throwing her pen-set at me. I went and sat in a blue leather chair with chromium arms. It felt, looked and smelled very much like a barber's chair.

In about half an hour a door opened beyond a bronze railing and two men came out backwards laughing. A third man held the door and echoed their laughter. They shook hands and the two men went away and the third man wiped the grin off his face in nothing flat and looked at Miss Van De Graaf. 'Any calls?' he asked in a bossy voice.

She fluttered papers and said: 'No, sir. A Mr – Dalmas to see you – from a Mr – West. His business is personal.'

'Don't know him,' the man barked. 'I've got more insurance than I can pay for.' He gave me a swift, hard look and went into his room and slammed the door. Miss Van De Graaf smiled at me with delicate regret. I lit a cigarette and crossed my legs the other way. In another five minutes the door beyond the railing opened again and he came out with his hat on and sneered that he was going out for half an hour.

He came through the gate in the railing and started for the entrance and then did a nice cutback and came striding over to me. He stood looking down at me – a big man, two inches over six feet and built to proportion. He had a well-massaged face that didn't hide the lines of dissipation. His eyes were black, hard, and tricky.

'You want to see me?'

I stood up, got out my billfold and gave him a card. He stared at the card and palmed it. His eyes became thoughtful.

'Who's Mr West?'

'Search me.'

He gave me a hard, direct, interested look. 'You have the right idea,' he said. 'Let's go into my office.'

The receptionist was so mad she was trying to initial three papers at once when we went past her through the railing.

The office beyond was long, dim and quiet, but not cool. There was a large photo on the wall of a tough-looking old bird who had held lots of noses to lots of grindstones in his time. The big man went behind about eight hundred dollars' worth of desk and tilted himself back in a padded high-backed director's chair. He pushed a cigar humidor at me. I lit a cigar and he watched me light it with cool, steady eyes.

Pair work

1 What do we know about John Dalmas by the end of this opening section?

2 Compare this extract with *The Reluctant Detective*: do they have some elements in common? You might consider the use of humour and the way people are described as starting points.

Group work

1 Look closely together at the moments when John Dalmas is speaking to or involved with the secretary, Miss Van der Graaf. Jot

down what you think each of them is thinking alongside what they actually do or say.

2   The subject matter of this extract is obviously American, but are there any other features of the writing that mark it out as from the USA? One way of looking closely might be to compare the passage with another one that seems very British, for example a piece from *The Necklace of Pearls*.

Written assignments

1   Try translating part of the extract into an English scene, making as many changes as you feel are necessary. Once you have written your 'translation' write a commentary about what has happened to the original in the process.

2   Imagine that a detective like John Dalmas or Philip Marlowe came to a small English country town as part of an investigation; write part of the story or treat it as a scene from a play or film.

Something the Cat Dragged In

Background notes

Patricia Highsmith was born in Texas in 1921, grew up in New York and has subsequently made her home in Europe. She is very well known in England for her stories which are often concerned with the macabre or the cruellest aspects of human behaviour. Many of her stories and novels have been adapted for film and television as they translate well from the page to the screen.

Group work

1   Do you all agree with the 'verdict'? Should the murder have been reported to the police so that the normal legal proceedings could have taken place? How would you have voted if you had been in the story. Consider the above questions together and then prepare a brief statement for the class putting forward your group decision.

2   Whatever the size of your group, take a character each and imagine how he or she would feel about the murder. Make sure you include Dickenson himself. Once you have heard each character's point of view consider whether you still agree or disagree with the final verdict.

3   Can murder ever be justified? Does the group feel that they know of any examples where someone has been 'justifiably killed'? From your

discussion select an example that gives the rest of the class a chance to think about this issue and see how they react.

4   Does Dickenson 'get away with it' because he is more upper class than Reeves? Are the characters in the story just siding with someone who they consider above them socially? Find evidence in the story to support your view.

Role play

Imagine that a local policeman asks to come to the Herbert's house the next day to make some inquiries about the disappearance of Bill Reeves. He or she is making routine enquiries at various houses in the area. Role play the discussion that the various characters have as they are deciding what to do when the police officer arrives. Will they reveal the truth this time?

Written assignments

1   Write your own view of the case, explaining whether you think that Dickenson should have been let off. Make sure you refer to the details of the story, so that you show where your ideas come from.

2   Phyllis thinks about the story that she will tell when she gets back home. Imagine that she has a close friend at home whom she decides to write to before her return because she is bursting to tell someone. Think carefully about Phyllis's character, her age and her part in the story and then write her letter.

3   Imagine that Dickenson falls under suspicion from the police about the disappearance of Reeves. Think of a likely reason, e.g. he gets drunk and partially reveals the story to someone in a pub or Reeves' body is found by someone out walking with a dog, etc. The police officer comes to the Herberts' house to interview everyone there because Dickenson was seen visiting them recently. You could write the scene using direct speech or in script form, as if from a play.

4   In this story the discovery of the hand led to the murder being uncovered. Use your imagination to think about some other strange discovery that might provide the basis for an exciting story. You might do this on your own or in collaboration with a partner.

If you decide to try and write a story with someone else then you will need to decide how you can best work together. Try talking through a number of ideas before deciding on your basic story-line. Once you have the idea will you actually write it together or divide up the writing in some way?

Superfluous Murder

Background notes

Milward Kennedy, who lived from 1894 until 1968, wrote both novels and short stories. He was a member of the Detection Club and a knowledgeable reviewer of crime fiction. He also wrote fiction under the name of Evelyn Elder. His stories often use humour at the expense of his character's best laid plans and this lightness of tone is reflected in the bloodless, non-violent nature of most of the deaths he portrays.

Pair work

What killed John Mansbridge? Decide together what was the cause of his death and then compare your view with that of another pair.

Group work

1 Detective stories often have a 'twist', sometimes several twists. Discuss together what you feel we mean by a 'twist' in a story and then consider if this story has one. Does it have one or more? Look closely at the text and if you feel there are twists pick them out and prepare an explanation of how they work for others in the class.
2 We see everything from John Mansbridge's point of view, but what do we know of his intended victim? Work together to produce a short description of Felix's character and also of John Mansbridge's motive. What did he have to gain from the murder?
3 If John Mansbridge had not died and had been tried for attempted murder what would your verdict as a jury be on what he did?

Written assignments

1 This story would be an intriguing one for a newspaper reporter to write up. Choose the style of a paper you know well and write a full article describing the case.
2 Imagine that both Felix and John kept personal diaries. Write the last few entries for one or both characters showing their thoughts and

feelings leading up to the night of the suicide/murder. Base your ideas closely on the evidence from the story.

3   Writing a clever story like this one is clearly a challenge. The reader has to be gripped by the story, but also surprised by what happens. Try writing a story which has a surprising twist and then ask some of the class to read it to see whether they think the twist works. You may want to spend some time thinking through the plot before you start. It may be helpful to talk through your ideas first and to prepare a chart showing crucial points in the plot development.

The Man with the Twisted Lip

Background notes

Sir Arthur Conan Doyle is famous for his creation of the great detective, Sherlock Holmes. The first story featuring this character appeared in 1891, and its immediate success allowed him to give up his struggle to succeed as an eye specialist. Conan Doyle lived from 1859 until 1930 and led a full and active life. He was a sportsman, he served as a doctor during the Boer War and was vigilant in the cause of British justice both as a detective and as a defender of the rights of the individual.

Group work

1   Sherlock Holmes and Doctor Watson are so well known that it is worth thinking about them *before* you read this story. Of all fictional detective heroes Sherlock Holmes has perhaps stood the test of time best. Working together jot down what you know about him and his assistant, Watson. How do you expect them to approach this case, what methods will Holmes use? Do you have any views on why he has remained such a popular figure?

2   All the clues in the story have been given by page 71. You and Holmes have all the evidence you need to solve the mystery. Once you reach the words 'A shock of very bright red hair grew low over his eyes and forehead,' stop and work together as a team to solve the mystery. Be systematic and pick out all the clues and list them. You could map out a flow chart of the events of the story showing what evidence exists at each key moment. Once you have worked out your solution, present it to the rest of the class before you all read on to the end and see if you were right!

Pair work

1 The story is several pages old before Holmes appears at all. Would it make any difference if it began with Holmes' first words and left out the previous pages?

Role play

Neville St Clair will have to meet his wife and explain everything to her. Role play this first meeting, preparing yourselves first by thinking through how each character must be feeling.

Written assignments

1 Write up Inspector Bradstreet's report of this case. Think about the kind of language he would use and the fact that he would have to include all the important details before summing everything up in his conclusion.

2 Imagine that Neville St Clair decides to prepare his wife for their meeting by writing to her explaining and justifying his behaviour; write his letter. If you prefer you could write about their meeting setting it out as a script.

3 The story not only deals with the issue of begging but also touches on opium addiction. Write an account of the problem of opium addiction as if you were a reporter in Victorian times. You may first want to find out some more information from the library and/or the History department about Victorian life.

4 The whole story is written in a very particular way: is it a difficult style to read? How can we tell when it was written? Try writing either a full story or perhaps an excerpt imitating the style of Sir Arthur Conan Doyle.

The Case for the Defence

Background notes

Graham Greene was born in 1904 and died in 1991. He was one of Britain's most prolific and highly esteemed novelists. Many of his novels and stories are concerned with crime though they often focus on the inner life of the criminal and the society which made him or her. His fiction, as you will see in *The Case for the Defence* asks the reader to confront their own ideas about major issues, such as the nature of guilt and innocence.

Group work

1 Was justice done at the end of the story? What does the group think?
2 The storyteller says 'Divine vengeance? I wish I knew.' Many people do believe in such an idea, do you? You need first of all to make sure that the class agrees on a definition of this difficult idea. Once you have agreement then you can start your group discussion. This is not a simple topic and you may not all think the same way. Perhaps you could begin with a question like 'Do criminals always get caught in the end?'

Pair work

Are you happy with the ending: does the story work for both of you? If it does, jot down your reasons why it seems a good ending. If you feel disappointed with it, then work out a different ending together in note form to explain to another pair and perhaps the class.

Role play

Work in a pair and act out a conversation between Mrs Salmon and a police officer. She has come to ask for help because she is afraid that the surviving twin (whether or not he is the murderer) will blame her for what happened and want revenge.

Written assignments

1 Continue the story from Mrs Salmon's point of view. Can she sleep at night?
2 The murderer, Adams, was clearly guilty and he would have got off because his lawyer cleverly used the twin brother to confuse the evidence. Rewrite the story from the lawyer's point of view. Think about his motives for taking on the case and the way he twisted the evidence. What kind of pressure was he under and what kind of person must he have been?
3 Take the same situation as *The Case for the Defence* and bring it up to date by bringing into the story the modern forensic technology that is used today to solve crimes. You might find it useful to talk this through with others first so that you can benefit from their suggestions. You

could think about methods like fingerprinting, analysis of blood stains, and the taking of fibre samples from clothes, carpets, etc.

Philomel Cottage

Background notes

Agatha Christie, who died in 1976, is often called 'The Queen of Crime' because of the vast number of ingeniously plotted novels and stories which she produced. Her detectives, Hercule Poirot and Miss Marple, are famous throughout the world and the novels which feature them have been successfully and extensively adapted for television and cinema. Her stories are very much a product of their time and of a particular class, but rise above these limits by their enduring ability to shock and surprise.

Pair work

☐ Who, or what, saves Alix?
☐ Is *Philomel Cottage* a good title?

Group work

1 Have a close look at the character of Alix. She manages to survive the whole ordeal remarkably well. Consider what we know about her at the beginning of the story and then what we have learnt by the end. What has been shown about her character?
2 Does the story succeed in keeping your interest? What does Agatha Christie do to try to build up suspense as the story develops? Work through the story together and try to agree on the places where the reader's suspicions are aroused or where there is a feeling that 'this must be important' about a particular detail. You could represent the plot as a chart showing each event and whether suspense increases or decreases as a result.

Role play

Imagine an interviewer comes from a woman's magazine to talk to Alix about her experiences. Role play the interview.

Written assignments

1   Adapt the story into either a radio or television drama, writing it out in script form and dividing it into scenes.

2   In some newspapers you will find obituaries, i.e. articles about famous people who have recently died. Using a combination of details from the story and your imagination write an obituary for Charles Lemaitre.

3   Imagine that Philomel Cottage becomes famous because of the way Alix defeated Charles Lemaitre and it develops into something of a tourist attraction. Write an entry for the local tourist guide describing it and the reasons why it is famous.

A Pair of Yellow Lilies

Background notes

Ruth Rendell was born in 1930. Her work has dominated English detective fiction in recent years because of her immense talent and versatility as a writer and the quality and quantity of her output. As with Highsmith and Christie, Rendell's work has been taken up enthusiastically by film makers and the stories featuring her Inspector Wexford are very popular on television. She is extremely interested in the exploration of individual motivation and in the heights and depths of human relationships.

Pair work

Do you think that Bridget has had a 'fair exchange' or should she have informed the police about what she discovered?

Role play

What will Bridget tell Elizabeth about her experience? Role play their next meeting.

Group work

1   Was the ending the one you expected? Look back together over the story and see what clues are given about the character of Patrick Baker.

2   Would you consider Bridget to blame for having her bag stolen. Was the whole episode simply her fault?

Discuss your views on these questions and prepare a brief statement for the class putting forward your group's conclusions.

Written assignments

1   Imagine that Elizabeth insists on Bridget informing the police about Patrick Baker. How do you think the police would set about dealing with this matter? Would they consider it important enough to act on or would they dismiss it as insignificant? Continue the story resolving this issue in what appears to you to be the likeliest way.

2   Bridget is an unlikely heroine but she and her new friend Elizabeth could make a strong team. Imagine that together they decide to teach Patrick Baker a lesson. Write about how they do this. You might prefer to invent your own character who, despite seeming very ordinary, turns out to be a hero or heroine in the end.

3   In some ways the story revolves around the recognition of a particular piece of clothing. Write your own story which involves a similar recognition.

A Wife in a Million

Background notes

Val McDermid is a journalist, novelist, playwright, Union official and short story writer whose work is currently published by The Women's Press. She lives and works in Manchester. The story, *A Wife in a Million* comes from the anthology *Reader, I Murdered Him*, a recent collection of short stories all written by women.

Group work

1   Discuss together as a group whether some or all of you worked out who the real killer was before it is revealed in the story? Who did you each suspect first and how did the writer manage to create and develop this suspicion? Looking carefully over the story again are there any clues or hints that you missed during your first reading?

2   Imagine that there has been a great public outcry about the deaths of all these innocent people and the newspapers and the general public are very keen to see the murderer tried and punished. It is up to the police whether they press charges or place Mrs Millfield in a mental hospital for treatment. Work together as a group of senior police

officers who have to review the case and then make a recommendation to their chief constable.

3 Work together as a group and consider the issue of unemployment. Should everyone have (a) the right to work or (b) should people be better prepared to spend periods of their working life without employment? Your task as a group is to decide whether you support (a) or (b). Prepare your ideas to present them to the class.

4 There is a hint in the story that Maggie has met some resistance in the police force because she is a woman. Do you think that this really happens? Once you have considered your views try to form a group statement in response to the following comment: 'As society is still unfair in its treatment of women, whenever a man and a woman are equally suited for a promotion then the woman should get the job'.

Role play

Choose either Bill Nicholson and Maggie or Maggie and Sarah and role play their next talk about the case and their feelings about the future.

Written assignments

1 Imagine that Sarah decides to write a detailed letter to one of the papers expressing her feelings about the supermarket murders and sympathy for the murderer. Choose a suitable newspaper and write her letter.

2 A few months after the case Maggie applies for promotion and Bill Nicholson has to write her reference. Think carefully about what you know of both characters and then write the reference.

3 Imagine that both Sarah and Maggie are invited to appear together on a television programme about women and crime. The programme will include police officers and ex-criminals. If they appear together then their relationship will become public knowledge and might possibly affect Maggie's career.

Write either one or two scenes as if from a play; the first one is Sarah and Maggie's discussion about whether to appear on television together or not; the second would be their interview at the television studio.

4 The story might be read as a kind of argument against unemployment. Take a topic you feel strongly about and put forward your views about it in the form of a story.

The Necklace of Pearls

Background notes

Dorothy L. Sayers lived from 1893 until 1957 and is perhaps most famous for her creation of the aristocratic amateur detective, Lord Peter Wimsey. In addition to short stories and novels she wrote plays, poetry, essays and translated the work of Dante into English. She became very knowledgeable about the genre of detective fiction and her work as an editor helped to establish and develop ideas about the form.

Group work

1 Are you a group of good detectives? Can you identify the exact moment in the story when Peter Wimsey realizes where the pearls are? Can you also work out how he decided to identify the villain? Work out your answers and then present them to the class.

2 Lord Peter Wimsey appears very frequently in Dorothy L. Sayers' writing and he is almost as well known as Sherlock Holmes. What qualities does he seem to have from your reading of this story? Do all fictional detectives have similar qualities?

Role play

Sir Septimus does not really want to invite the police to his own house but neither does he want Comphrey to get away without punishment. Role play the conversation between Sir Septimus and Peter Wimsey when they try to decide what steps to take with Comphrey.

Written assignments

1 Can you turn this story into a puzzle for others? The story is full of evidence about the characters, where they come from, what they have in their pockets, possible motives for the crime and so on. How could you organize the story to challenge readers at different stages of their reading? Write a guide to the story which invites readers to stop and review the evidence at various stages.

2 A television producer wants to use this story for a 'Christmas Special' show but thinks that the events are too brief and that there is not enough intrigue for a modern audience. He has asked you to expand on the story using the same situation and characters. He wants you either to write an explanation of how you would do it or a page or two of sample script.

3   Lord Peter Wimsey moves in a very particular kind of aristocratic world. Write another story featuring him and try to create the kind of scene which is found in *The Necklace of Pearls*. Have a close look at the descriptive details of the story before you begin your own. For example consider the wealthy and luxurious settings, the aristocratic manner of characters' speech and so on.

Extended Activities

This collection offers you a chance to think about the many and various ways in which crime and detection stories are written. This section aims to help you think about and write about groups of stories and about ideas to do with this particular subject.

1   What are crime and detection stories? Have a look at all the stories you have read and work out some of their important features. You could do this through designing a grid with columns for features and the titles of each story down the side. You might have headings like detective/investigator, male/female characters, type of crime, type of plot, setting and so on.

2   You might look closely at the way crime writers play with their readers' expectations. For example, if there is to be a final twist, we have to expect something different but still be convinced that the surprise at the end was always possible. You will need to look very closely at how different writers achieve this.

3   Crime writing is immensely popular. Can you explain what makes it so fascinating, using examples from the stories here as well as your own reading and viewing?

4   Is Crime writing full of macho men and women who-need-to-be-saved or is it more complex than that? What have you noticed about the portrayal of men and women in these stories?

5   Crime stories reflect the age they are written in, but have they really changed much since the time of Sherlock Holmes?

6   Several stories in this collection involve murder or attempted murder: have these stories helped you to understand some of the motives and causes of murder?

7   A number of stories feature the classic detective figure. What characteristics make up one of these investigative heroes? Is there something about them that we all want to imitate?

8   Do you think a strong interest in reading and watching Crime stories could be a bad thing?

9   Which stories in the collection go well together? Choose examples of pairs of stories that have an interesting similarity or contrast in the way they are written. For example you might compare Sherlock Holmes and Lord Peter Wimsey as detectives, *Something the Cat Dragged In* and *Superfluous Murder* as murder stories, or the way the mind of a murderer is portrayed in *Philomel Cottage* and *A Wife in a Million*.

Wider Reading

This section provides you with some suggestions for further reading and also some ideas for assignments on this reading that you might want to use as a part of your work at school.

Assignments

The following are general suggestions for work.

1 Read the stories or novels of any individual author who has interested you and trace his or her development as a Crime fiction writer.

2 Select two crime novels by different authors that might be compared by theme or subject matter.

3 How do male and female Crime writers compare? Choose one text from a female and one from a male author and see if you think there are genuine differences in the way they write about men, women and crime.

4 Choose a range of texts and use them to define what good Crime writing means to you.

The Simple Art of Murder, Raymond Chandler, Houghton Mifflin, 1950
The Labours of Hercules, Agatha Christie, Fontana, 1961
The Listerdale Mystery, Agatha Christie, Fontana 1961
The Adventures of Sherlock Holmes, Sir Arthur Conan Doyle, (1892), Penguin Books, 1981
The Penguin Complete Sherlock Holmes, Sir Arthur Conan Doyle, Penguin Books
Reader, I Murdered Him, ed. Jen Green, The Women's Press Ltd., 1989
Chillers, Patricia Highsmith, Penguin Books, 1989
Collected Short Stories, Ruth Rendell, Arrow Books, 1988
Hangman's Holiday, Dorothy L. Sayers, New English Library, 1974
Great Tales of Detection, ed. Dorothy L. Sayers, J. M. Dent & Sons, 1936
Penguin Classic Crime, ed. Julian Symons, Penguin Books, 1988